Josephus Daniels

**The First Fallen Hero**

a biographical sketch of Worth Bagley, ensign, U.S.N.

Josephus Daniels

**The First Fallen Hero**
*a biographical sketch of Worth Bagley, ensign, U.S.N.*

ISBN/EAN: 9783337190866

Printed in Europe, USA, Canada, Australia, Japan

Cover: Foto ©Andreas Hilbeck / pixelio.de

More available books at **www.hansebooks.com**

# The First...
## ...Fallen Hero

A BIOGRAPHICAL SKETCH OF

## WORTH BAGLEY,
### ENSIGN, U. S. N.

—— BY

## JOSEPHUS DANIELS.

---

He gave his life for his Country on the Torpedo boat Winslow in Cardenas Bay, May 11th, 1898.

---

"And thus this man died, leaving his death for an example of a noble courage, and a memorial of virtue, not only unto young men, but unto all his nation."—2nd. Maccabees, vi, 31.

---

NORFOLK, VA.:
SAM W. BOWMAN,
PUBLISHER.

COPYRIGHTED 1898 BY SAM W BOWMAN.

# PREFACE.

IN response to a request made to the family of Ensign Worth Bagley for a sketch of his life for publication, this volume has been prepared. There has been no attempt to write an elaborate biography, but only a desire to put in permanent form, for the emulation of aspiring youth, the record of the short and brilliant career of the first American officer to die in battle in the war between the United States and Spain.

The editor has sought to let the letters of the dead Ensign tell the story of his young life. During the eight and a half years that elapsed between his entering the Naval Academy and his heroic death at Cardenas, his letters to his mother, sisters and brothers touched upon every topic that interested him. They give a better insight to his hopes, his loves, his ambitions and his character than can be derived from any other source. Written for the eye only of those he loved best there is no reserve. The extracts given show his inmost thoughts and feelings. It is only from such letters that the real heart of the man can be known.

In collating from the letters written home by Worth Bagley, and the letters of sympathy to his sorrowing mother, the controlling purpose has been to convey a clear understanding of his sweet home life; his abounding love for his mother; his affection for his sisters, brothers and kindred; his high ideals of life; his chivalry that shone out in all his association with women; his clean and pure life—

> "His strength was as the strength of ten
> Because his heart was pure;"

his manly spirit and steadfastness of purpose, his generous disposition, comradeship and broad charity; his noble ambitions, animating to high and lofty deeds; his devotion to his profession to which he was wedded; his love for his fellow men and his faith in God; and his splendid courage, enabling him to conquer fear and meet death with a smile upon his face.

It is hoped and believed that, though the preparation has been hurried, the simple recital of what he thought and what he did will stimulate to high aims and lofty aspirations all manly and ambitious youth who are moved by the example of heroic achievement.

J. D.

# The First Fallen Hero.

## CHAPTER I.

### BIRTH AND BOYHOOD.

"Easter Monday was a visiting day of some importance at the house of a Grand Master in this city. The little Odd Fellow weighed nine pounds and three-quarters. Long may the little Grand Master wave!"

THIS was the announcement of the birth of Worth Bagley, which appeared in the Raleigh News in its issue of April 7th, 1874. He was born in Raleigh, N. C., on the sixth day of April 1874, in the house in which his mother now resides, on the corner of Blount and South streets. His father at the time was Grand Master of Odd Fellows of the State of North Carolina, and it was his prominence in the order that caused the editor to call "the little stranger" an Odd Fellow.

Worth Bagley's ancestry was honorable. His ancestors gave abundant evidence of their patriotism in peace and in war. He was the oldest son of the late Maj. Wm. H. Bagley, a native of Perquimans County, North Carolina. When the War Between the States was declared, Maj. Bagley volunteered in the first company for the Confederate service that was raised in his county, having, prior to the war edited "The Sentinel" at Elizabeth City, and having obtained license to practice law in 1859. He was at first commissioned Lieutenant and afterwards Captain, transferred to Company A. 8th., Shaw's Regiment, Clingman's Brigade, and he followed the fortunes of the Confederacy in the uniform of the gray to the end, except when as a prisoner on parole at home in 1864, he was elected and served in the State Senate. He was afterwards made Major of the 68th. N. C. Regiment, of which Hon. E. C. Yellowley of Pitt county was Colonel, and held that position in the Confederate army when Lee surrendered. In civil life, he was elected and served as Register of Deeds of Perquimans county before he was of age. In July 1865, President Andrew Johnson tendered him the appointment as Superintendent of the U. S. Mint at Charlotte, but he could not take the "iron clad" oath and could not accept that office. Upon the election of Jonathan Worth as Governor in 1865 he became Private Secretary to the Governor, and in March 1866 he married the Governor's daughter, Adelaide Anne. From this union there are now living five children, Addie Worth, wife of Josephus Daniels, Belle Worth, Ethel, William Henry and David Worth. In 1868 Maj. Bagley was chosen Clerk of the Supreme Court of North Carolina which position he held until his death, February 21st, 1886. He was an active Odd Fellow all his life, serving in every position in the gift of that order. In 1873 he was Grand Master of the State, and in 1874, 1875, 1876, 1877 he was chosen Grand Representative of the Sovereign Grand Lodge of the World. He was also a member of the Masonic order and of the Royal Arcanum. Major Bagley was a son of Col. Willis H. Bagley, a highly respected citizen who was sheriff of Perquimans county for many years. His grandfather, William Bagley, fought in the War of 1812, and was at the battle of "Crany's Island," Norfolk Harbor. His great-grandfather, Thomas Bagley, served in the Revolutionary War. His mother was Mary Elizabeth Clary, who was directly descended from Mackrora Scarborough, who was Colonel of "His Majesty's Militia," member of the Colonial Legislature, and of the Governor's Council.

Ensign Bagley's mother is the youngest living daughter of the late Governor Jonathan Worth and Martitia Daniel, daughter of John Daniel of Charlotte county, Virginia. She was a granddaughter of Col. Archibald Murphy, who was a colonel in the Revolutionary Army. The Worths were originally Quakers and were among the first of the Friends who came to America primarily for the purpose of finding in the New World a place where they could worship God according to the dictates of conscience They settled at Nantucket before the coming over to Pennsylvania of the colony of Friends under Wm. Penn. William Worth, who emigrated from Devonshire, England, to this country in or about 1640, was the common progenitor of Gen. William Jenkins Worth, of Mexican war fame, and Governor Jonathan Worth, grandfather of Ensign Worth Bagley. His Worth ancestry dates back to the reign of Cromwell. The first emigrants to America settled in Massachusetts, and between 1771 and 1775, Daniel Worth, the founder of the North Carolina family, with others of the Society of Friends, moved to Guilford county. His son, Dr. David Worth, a physician and farmer, who was born at Centre Church, Guilford county, in 1776, was the great-grandfather of Worth Bagley.

The Worths have long been leaders in law, business and politics in North Carolina. Worth Bagley's grandfather, Jonathan Worth, first entered public life as a member of the House of Commons in 1830. He was elected again in 1840 and was a State Senator in 1858-59, and 1860-61. In that body he vehemently opposed secession, "voting against submitting the question of a Convention (even to consider the matter of taking the State out of the Union) to the people; and, the Legislature deciding against him, addressing a circular to his constituents, advising them to vote against Convention, as the surest way of defeating secession. * * After secession, he gave in his adhesion to the *de facto* Government, and acted toward it in the same good faith which distinguished all his conduct, public and private." In 1862-63 he was a member of the House of Commons and was elected Public Treasurer of the State: he was re-elected without opposition in 1864, and held the position until the then State Government was overthrown by the Federal forces in 1865. President Johnson appointed him State Treasurer, but he resigned in a short time to become a candidate for Governor against Provisional-Governor Holden. He was elected and entered upon the duties of Governor on the 28th day of December, 1865. He was re-elected Governor in 1866. He continued in the Executive office until July, 1868, when the government was suspended by that organized under the Reconstruction Acts of Congress. He surrendered the position, writing a protest denying the constitutionality of those Acts of Congress and the legality of his removal. He died on the 5th day of September, 1869.

Worth Bagley was a robust and healthy child, growing in strength and manly grace, and as a lad possessed a gentleness and courtesy that was the delight of his parents and instructors.

Speaking of his home, on the occasion of his last visit to Raleigh, he said, "I have always been happy here. It is the sweetest place in the world to me." Growing up in a happy home where love and unselfishness reigned, he was as chivalrous toward his sisters and playmates while wearing kilts as he was gallant and courteous in his intercourse with men and women in the clubs and brilliant gatherings in which afterwards he was a favorite guest. There was in him the rare blending of the simplicity and directness of his Quaker ancestry and the bonhommie and geniality that is the characteristic of Southern civilization. He would not contend, even as a little child, for his own with his sisters or girl playmates, but he surrendered to no boy in any contest and, while almost wholly free from school-boy fighting, he stood up for his rights against all comers. If this led to a fight, he did not shirk it, but fought to the finish having the creed: "You must always stand up for your rights and let nobody run over you." That was his spirit—to encroach on the rights of no one and to permit no encroachment upon his rights. "He had an inherent sense of justice and fair play," said one of his school-mates, "and I do not recall any fight he ever had at school except when he took the part of a smaller boy against a big boy who was imposing on the little fellow. After he took part, it was his quarrel and he did not quit until he came out on top."

The oldest son of a family of six children, he was very dear to his father, who entered into the lives and thoughts of his children, drawing them out and helping them with perfect understanding of their powers. The letters between father and son illustrate the strong bond between them.

The following little jingle, written in the form of a letter to please a child's fancy, was sent to Worth when he was five years old:

RALEIGH, December 7th, 1879.
DEAR WORTH:

I drop you a line, as I have time, to let you know what is the go; 'tis Sunday now, and just somehow, I thought to you I'd write, to see if not you've me forgot—to tell you, too, what will be true, if, by Tuesday night, you do not write.

The clouds are gone, the rain is done and everything is bright; the sun shines out and, all about, there is nothing but it's light. Addie and Belle both are well, and so is "Henry boo"; little Ethel's neat and very sweet, and so is Edwin, too. Mama is good and Papa's mood is on the good incline; so be not sad and only glad, and bear us all in mind.

Surely give Sis a loving kiss, from each and every one, and let her, too, a kiss give you, my darling little son. Cousin Henry kiss, and his little sis, also, the "little wee," Aunt Annie squeeze and Uncle teaze ; and, then a good boy be. Now do not fail, by Tuesday's mail, to us to send a letter ; for if you do—my word is true—I tell you, you had better !
Affectionately,
PAPA.

The son was not less thoughtful. The following letter, written at the age of seven years to his father, on the latter's birthday, discloses his generous desires which were early developed :

JACKSON, N. C., July 5th, 1881.
DEAR PAPA :
Please send me some torpedoes and some pop-crackers, I cannot send you a present. Henry Benton and I are going down to the brick kiln to see what our boats are doing. I cannot find you a present.
Every time Sizzie says "March," me and Henry Benton do like we are marching. Your son,
WORTH BAGLEY.

Among many other letters written to his cousins as a boy, three extracts are given :

May 11th, '81 : "Miss Nettie Marshall calls me her best adder."

Aug. 16th, '81 : "I lost my bird betting with ———. I wont bet any more. It is wrong I believe."

June 3rd, '88 : "Eighteen speeches were made at Morson & Denson's Academy Commencement. Mine was the very last, and when I got up, I tell you I was scared. But I got through all right and got more boquets than any other boy. After it was all over people crowded around me congratulating, as they said. I got mortally tired of it.........I got five 'honors', three of them were 'firsts' and two were 'seconds'. The 'firsts' were on Latin Exercises, Algebra, Penmanship. The 'seconds' were on Latin Grammar, Latin Reading. The 'first honor' is given to the boy who stands the best examination in his class, the 'second honor' is given to the next best."

On February 21st, 1886, after a long illness, Major Bagley died. When the twelve year old boy recovered from the first blow, the sense of his responsibility as the oldest son gave him the fortitude of a man. He hid his own grief to be able to comfort and cheer the widowed mother, and from the hour that she leaned upon his strong young arm for support, in the anguish of her woe, until the fateful day at Cardenas, he was her strength and stay. On the afternoon of the funeral of his father, as they stood by the open grave, his mother felt an arm about her neck. It was Worth's arm and his hand was affectionately patting her face. Coming home he said, "Mother, lean on me and I will take care of you." A few months after the death of her husband, Mrs. Bagley took her youngest son to her church (the Presbyterian) to have him

baptized. As with his hand in hers, she approached the altar she
found that Worth was by her side, standing in the place made vacant
by his father's death. It was his own thought and it brought a feeling
of happiness into the saddened life of the mother that could have
come from no other human source. She came more and more to
lean upon him and to find comfort and help in his strong arm, his
brave spirit his true heart, his stimulating hope and faith. To
his sisters, to whom he had ever been considerate, a gentler sympathy was shown, and, feeling the responsibility of his example
toward his younger brothers, he became to them an example of
filial affection, respect, courtesy and obedience. The loss of his
father while it was not permitted to cloud the cheerfulness of
his sweet home life, gave him the steadying sense of duty, and
made him older and more studious. He early became a Christian, joining the First Presbyterian Church in Raleigh, on the 28th
of November 1887. having been baptized when a young child in
that church.

Of his school days, before going to the Naval Academy his
teachers are the most competent ones to speak. Among the very
first to write to his stricken mother was Mrs. E. McDonald who
was his teacher at the age of six years when he first became a pupil in the Centennial Graded school at Raleigh. Writing from
Winston she said :

"How my heart goes out in sympathy, for you and yours, at the loss
of your noble boy. I, his first teacher, have ever remembered him with
love and affection, and watched, with pride, his successful career, and
to-day mingle my tears with yours in this hour of trial."

Mrs. J. M. Barbee, who had been his teacher at the Centennial
Graded School at one time, said :

"Worth was very popular as a school boy and had wit and gallantry.
He was even then fond of ships. When a pupil of Miss Gales, he drew
a picture of a full-rigged vessel and wrote under it, 'It takes fair Gales
to drive my ship.'"

Prof. E. P. Moses, of Rock Hill, S. C., who was superintendent
of the Raleigh Graded Schools, writing to Mrs. Bagley, said :

"The fact that Worth was a student of mine and always such a noble
boy, makes the loss a personal one to me. It will be a comfort to you to
feel that his heroism in life was as conspicuous as his heroism in death,
which has won the admiration of a whole nation."

There is still preserved by his mother an Easter card, presented
in March, 1884, as a prize, by Miss Jean Gales, his teacher at the

FROM ONE TO TWENTY-ONE.

Centennial Graded School, on which is written:

"Prize received by Worth Bagley for spelling thirty words correctly. The words were selected and prize awarded by the editor of the Teacher."

In a letter written in his eleventh year, while visiting an aunt in the country, he wrote his mother:

"I can swim 150 feet."

His ability to swim was afterwards worth a great deal to him when he entered the Naval Academy. Writing from the same place, during the same visit his interest in athletics and his spirit of pleasantry are thus shown:

"Tell Henry I hope Cain, the new pitcher, will be able (Abel) to shut out the Wilmington club when they play at Charlotte..... I understand now what piscatorial means, as I have studied Latin..... I wonder if I am included in Miss——'s love. She said she sent it to all the family."

Finishing the course at the Centennial Graded School, he entered the classical school of Morson & Denson, at Raleigh in 1884, to prepare for college. He took a high stand there, winning medals and honors in a class composed of many young men of talent, some of whom have already made reputations. Prof. Hugh Morson, one of the principals of the school writes of his pupil:

"Worth Bagley was for several years a pupil of mine, and as one who taught, knew and loved him, it may not be amiss at this time when his native city and state are filled with mingled feelings of grief at the loss of a son so brave and gifted, and with pride at his heroic death, to say a few words in tribute to his many noble qualities of heart and head. He entered the Raleigh Male Academy at the opening of the session of 1886, and was until he went to Annapolis, a pupil of the school, pursuing such studies mainly as were preparatory to a classical course at college. As might be supposed, he was always a leader among his school-fellows, beloved, respected, and looked up to by them all; and as his nature was pure, honest and truthful, scorning everything false and base, he ever exerted a healthful and beneficial influence upon the moral tone of the school. In all athletic games and sports he displayed surprising skill and strength for his age, and showed those same qualities of daring and endurance which afterwards won such reputation for him as an athlete in the games played at the Naval Academy with West Point and other institutions.

"As a pupil he was studious, obedient and faithful In the discharge of duty, with a character above reproach and intellectual endowments of a very high order. As evidence of this, at the close of the session of 1888-89, he received the highest honors in several of his classes, and was fully prepared, though only fifteen years of age, to take, as he intended, the full classical course at the University of North Carolina; but entering a competitive examination for appointment to the U. S. Naval Academy at Annapolis, he won the prize in a large class from this district composed of young men who were all his seniors by several years. The committee who held this examination reported to Representative Bunn that 'young Bagley's papers' were almost perfect."

Capt. C. B. Denson, a co-principal of the school, writes:

"At the Raleigh Male Academy he excelled in classical studies, and at the age of fifteen years was prepared to enter the University. His character was lofty and noble; he scorned petty things; generous, warm-hearted, resolute, and brave. As a student he mastered everything thoroughly; to him duty was the supreme watchword. He was strikingly handsome, with fine open frankness of the sailor. His friends here may be said to have numbered the whole people, who looked with pride to his future advancement."

The News and Observer in its report of Morson and Denson's closing exercises in 1888, said:

"Master Worth Bagley showed wonderful oratorical powers and talent in delivering "The South of the Past and Present." He surprised his young friends who applauded him liberally and heartily."

From earliest boyhood he read with avidity the war-like periods in history, and though fond of all manly sports, he was a voracious reader, spending hours at the time reading historic novels as well as those histories that gave the most graphic pictures of war and revolution. He knew how every great decisive battle of the world had been fought and won and before he was old enough to leave off short pants his knowledge of the ships of the navy and his interest in the life of Paul Jones, Farragut, Lord Nelson and other great naval commanders was marked.

As I write there lie before me portions of the manuscript of a story of a naval encounter in the fogs off Newfoundland, written when he was about thirteen years old. Though the production of a school-boy, written on Saturdays, it shows that at that early age he was familiar with nautical terms and naval battles. His family believed that he had real talent and encouraged him to fit himself for a career as author of sea tales and naval methods. He had a fine imagination, wrote readily and elegantly, was a master of good English, and the plot of his school-boy novel of the sea gives promise that he would have made reputation as an author and a novelist.

As he grew older, the ambition to go into the navy fired him, and when in 1889, Hon. Benjamin H. Bunn, at that time Member of Congress from the Fourth Congressional District, gave notice that he would appoint as cadet to Annapolis the youth who stood the best competitive examination, the desire to win the appointment stimulated him to thorough preparation for the contest. Mr. Bunn named as the committee to conduct the examination, Prof. A. G. Wilcox, of Nash, chairman, Prof. E. W. Kennedy, of Durham, and Prof. Purington, of Wake Forest College. There were a number of applicants who presented themselves for examination. After standing this competitive examination and before knowing the result, he went in June, 1889, to the University of North Carolina, where he passed the entrance examination, and in June wrote to his youngest sister,

"I got a letter from Chapel Hill the other day saying I had passed the entrance examinations So I can enter the University even if I can't enter Annapolis."

A few days thereafter, in another letter to the same sister in playful mood he signed himself, "Worth Bagley, U. S. N., Lord High Admiral to His Majesty Ben Harrison's fleet."

When, after marking all the papers, the committee announced that Worth Bagley had been the successful applicant, his joy knew no bounds. The appointment was dated June 30th, 1889. Always self contained, even as a boy, his enthusiasm could not now be suppressed. It pervaded the household and family circle. Soon thereafter, in order to be fully prepared to stand his entrance examination at the Naval Academy, he went to Annapolis to study for one month under a special instructor. During that preparation, it chanced that being in Annapolis with his oldest sister, just at the close of the examination, the writer recalls the joyous pride of the noble young fellow as he bounded across the campus to tell his loving sister of his success and to cheer her heart by saying, jestingly, in the flush of his first victory, "I will be an Admiral one of these days." To this hour I can see the fresh and glowing young face, made truly beautiful with the light of conscious strength and illuminating ambition.

When he went to Annapolis to take private lessons to prepare for his entrance examination, his mother wrote to the instructor:

"Worth has always been a studious boy and has been fortunate enough to gain the regard of his teachers. He is free from any bad habits."

This was not merely a mother's partiality that thus told of his good habits and deportment. It was what his playmates and all who knew him could have truthfully written of the pure-hearted young lad, who through life, retained the qualities that gave him the friendship of the best men and women wherever his duty and pleasure called him.

From his entrance into the Naval Academy, he was no longer an inmate of the home-circle, except during holidays and vacations, but no anniversary of any member of the household escaped him and he wrote frequent letters and made long stays at home whenever leave was allowed him. He loved his home with a passion that made him long for the periodical vacations when he could rest under the shades where he had played as a boy, and he always hurried home so as not to lose a day from the sweet communion with his family. He kept in touch with his schoolmates and friends, too, and had a deep and abiding attachment for, and growing pride in, his native city and state. His state pride was based upon a knowledge of its glorious history, the sturdy patriotism of its people, and the simple virtues that distinguish them.

## CHAPTER II.

### AT THE NAVAL ACADEMY.

Mrs. W. H. Bagley,
    Raleigh, N. C.
        Annapolis, Md., Sept. 7th, 1889.

Passed mentally and physically.
                      Worth Bagley.

THIS telegram, which his mother has preserved, announced the fulfilment of his youthful ambition. He was but a few months more than fifteen years old, the youngest member of his class, and much younger than the average entrance age at the Academy. He had given special attention at school to the classics, and was a fine Greek and Latin scholar. The course at Annapolis was so different, leaving out Greek and Latin altogether, and giving mathematics, chemistry and kindred subjects first place, that the young cadet found it required very hard work to keep up with his class, composed mainly of older boys who had been trained with a view to the studies taught at the Academy. His letters home for the first year or more tell of his application to his studies, his "boning" to keep up on "skinny" and the other studies that required all his attention. Sometimes he wrote that it was almost too hard, but these expressions were accompanied by an expressed determination to do his best. There ran through them all a yearning for home, a tender love for home folks and a desire to so act as to win the commendation of his mother. A few extracts from letters to his mother will serve to show the channel of his thoughts:

Feb. 23rd, '90. "You never wrote me whether I was behind hand in my Bible or not. I am now nearly through Job."

March 23rd, '90: Tell David a good way to learn to spell is to ask what signs and bills read on the street and spell them over to himself. Do you remember how I used to spell "Little Joker Smoking Tobacco?"
......... Ethel must not be discouraged with Cæsar as the first book is very much harder than any of the others and after awhile one becomes used to his style and reads him without difficulty. When I was in Virgil I could read Cæsar without opening a vocabulary and anybody can do the same thing. I know she will like French; it is very easy to understand after awhile. We in our class can understand the native Frenchmen in that department very easily when they talk."

June 1st, '90: "Do be careful about yourself. Don't work any now for a long time. You positively *must not* while you are having these headaches. Rest a lot."

June 8th, '90: "We have been having a good time during the past week. The board of visitors has been here........ A cadet fell overboard The Admiral then had us called aft again and gave us a speech in which he mentioned the cadet falling overboard, saying that his catching the rope showed the cool-headedness cadets acquire while here. He ended by saying that in after life whenever we should find ourselves in any strait whatever always clutch with one hand high up on the nearest rope for ourselves, and with the other hand still higher for the government. I heard a pretty wild fellow in my class say: 'Government be d—— if ever I fall overboard.'"

Dec. 12th, '90: "I hope you received my letter on your birthday as it was a 25 pager.........I wish I had been home with you. A thousand hugs and kisses."

Oct. 1st, '90: Whenever I get homesick I get out my photo album and think of home. Your letters are so sweet and encouraging that they make me nearly cry in the midst of my rough surroundings."

Oct 7th, '90: "I read my Bible every night. Last night I read the 14th chapter of Isaiah. Where are you?'"

Oct. 26th, '90: "Your letter came last night when I was in my despondent mood and it was so long and home-like that it made me feel entirely different .... I like to get a letter on Sunday when I come back from church. But I would like to get them at all hours of the day."

Dec. 7th, '90: "I enjoyed the Thanksgiving box you sent. I enjoyed the butter and biscuit about as much as anything else. Of all the orange cakes you have sent me that was the best. None of the people in this building had ever eaten any to compare with it, or ever will unless they get your receipt."

Dec. 7th, '90: "I generally take my photograph album down at night when I havn't had any letters for several days and gaze and gaze at all the familiar faces. It seems to keep off homesickness."

Dec. 21st, '90: "I am so glad of the prospect of going home that I am just wild for Wednesday to come so I can go. You must hang up my stocking Christmas eve so I can get it when I come at 2 o'clock Christmas."

Jan. 19th, '91: "A new preacher preached at our church to-day and I was delighted with the sermon, which was directed principally to young men, as the State Y. M. C. A. meets here this week. His text was "Serving the Lord." He made one point which struck me very much. He said that it is not to be saved that we serve the Lord, but because we are saved. I was taught several things by his sermon and realized more than ever how hard and difficult it is to live up to our vows. I always feel the need of strength of purpose and will, and nearly all of us do I guess ........ I know there is but one way to get this strength and I always pray for it."

Jan. 10th, '91: (When his niece was born, he wrote:) "Ever since I heard it I have been very glad and jubilant. Kiss Addie a thousand times for me and tell her I have a great notion to try to get sick leave just to go home and see the baby. I bet $50. she is not any more proud of it than I am. You failed to tell me the weight of the young one and the color of her hair. Love to all and a thousand kisses for my darling sweetheart mother."

Jan. 25th, '91: "I have been rejoicing and feeling better lately in my heart. I had begun to feel cold in my religion for awhile, but lately I have had all my love for Christ, and a desire to serve Him, return to me. I have felt light hearted and glad lately and I attribue it greatly to this. I had begun to pray in my bed at night and I think we might as well not pray at all as to do that."

May 1st, '91: (Writing to his oldest sister:) "I guess you are treating X like you treated us both that time we had the mumps. I tell you I wish I could have that sort of mumps again."

Feb. 22nd, '91: "I didn't know what hard studying meant until I struck this second term.........I have been thinking several days about papa, and I feel and have felt during this year so many times how I wished I could have him with me and that we all could be here together ........I am getting old I tell you. Only a month and I will be 17. Just think of that! I am so glad that you are reading "The Light that Failed" I thought it was really beautiful."

March 29th, '91: "I wouldn't swap places for anything. Riches are not *all* in this world."

April 19th, '91: "...... never hears from his mother but once a week and I don't see how in the world he can stand it."

April 12th, '91: "Tell Aunt Julia that I may be a little more dignified, but the same boy that used to trot around in bare legs, and just as innocent and tries to be as pure as the little boy who used to draw the sled and help build the fires to drive off the sand flies."

Among the incidents of his life at Annapolis which illustrate his character, there is one that stands out conspicuous. It was shortly after he had entered the Academy that some of the upper classmen entered his room and "hazed" him. The authorities had determined to stamp out hazing at any cost and to expel those who practiced it. Somehow it became known that Cadet Bagley had been "hazed" and he was summoned before the Commandant and ordered to give the names of the "hazers". An account of this experience is thus related:

"I have been taught", he said, "that it is dishonorable to tell on a playmate or schoolmate. I mean no disrespect to or disobedience of authority, but I would regard myself as doing a dishonorable act if I were to tell. That I cannot do." The Commandant said, "Unless you obey orders and tell you will have to go on the Santee". (The Santee was the ship on which cadets were sent for severe punishment.) He persisted in his refusal and for eighteen days he was kept in confinement on the Santee, being permitted to leave it only to go to his recitations, and then being allowed to speak only to his instructors. At the end of that time the cadets who had hazed him confessed and asked for his release. He would have remained in prison indefinitely before he would have told who hazed him, such was his devotion to what he considered honorable."

In the Spring of 1891, the fear that had haunted him for weeks, that he might not successfully pass the examination, was realized. Upon the examination his mark was 2:42 when 2:50 was required. Failing to obtain a re-examination, he wrote his mother a frank and manly letter, stating all the circumstances and expressing the hope that Hon. B. H. Bunn, member of Congress from the Fourth North Carolina District; by whom he had originally been appointed, would see his way clear to re-appoint him. The devoted mother took the letter to Mr. Bunn, who immediately made out the papers of re-appointment, and with a grateful heart, she wrote to her son of his good fortune. As soon as he heard the news, the following letter written from Annapolis was sent to Mr. Bunn. The date does not appear, but it was in June, 1891.

MY DEAR MR. BUNN:

My mother has written to me of your kindness to her and me in granting me a re-appointment to the Naval Academy. I have never thought that it is the part of the fallen to make excuses, but I feel that I must tell you............ I hope that with the start that I now have and the determination to fulfil every duty that lies in my way, I shall never cause you to regret the appointment you have made. I shall never forget and shall always appreciate your great kindness, and shall try, by hard work and study, to show myself worthy of being a North Carolinian and your appointee. Believe me, Sir,

With much respect,
Gratefully yours,
WORTH BAGLEY.

At the same time he wrote to his mother, calling her "My Dearest Little Mother," from which a long extract is taken:

"The first thing I thought when I found that I was not to have a re-examination was, not as to how I was ever to get or rather finish my education, but how it might hurt my dearest mother and sweet, dear home folks. I was so afraid that it had gone badly with you that it was a long time before I could summon courage to ask —— how you took it. I thought to myself, if I have caused my own mother a single gray hair I will be wretched indeed. I don't think I have ever caused you trouble knowingly and I hope so much that this affair will not go hard with you. But now that I have a new appointment I will stand so high that my mama will be laughing instead of crying soon.

"I was so rejoiced when I received ——'s letter saying that Mr. Bunn had re-appointed me, that my heart leaped and I felt like going and telling everybody. My classmates have all congratulated me on it and nearly all have expressed the opinion that I will do finely when I re-enter and that I attempted it too early in my life. I know they are right, and, with the experience I have had, the lessons I have learned, and the determination and ambition that seem to have returned anew to me, I am certain I will take an honorable stand in my new class. It will be the first time that I have not been the youngest man in my class in my life. But, my dear mother, if you knew what desire I have to redeem myself, you would be as sure as I am that I will study faithfully and stand high, and who knows but what I shall stand among the 'fiends' and come home with a star on my collar! [This ambition was realized and he came home with a star on his collar.—EDITOR.] So be happy and then I will be happy too.... I think that all of my late troubles (the first set-back I ever had) have aged me in many respects, and I believe firmly they have done me a great deal of good and have taught me many lessons. Perhaps for this reason, God put the punishment upon me. For whatever reason He did put it upon me I know it is for the best because He did it and He has been good to us all If I could feel that you are in anyway satisfied with me it certainly would make me feel glad."

Writing to his mother July 19th, 1891, he said, referring to two relatives he loved very much:

"I was so glad to see them that I didn't know what to do. I guess no one would have noticed, though, that I was so glad, because I never go into any outward display of showing my love for anyone. I never believe in kissing and kissing and telling persons how glad you are to see them. I can meet anyone cordially, but if they can't know and find out by my actions that I am glad to see them why then I don't want them to know it at all. It is the same way about loving a person, with me. I don't believe in telling them thousands and thousands of times how much you love them, but show in your actions that you love them and act so that they may find it out."

Upon his re-entrance in the Academy in the fall of 1891, he became a member of the class of '95 in which he graduated. From his re-entrance until graduation his life ran smoothly, bringing realization of his ambitions, delightful vacations at home where his presence was a joy and a light, cruises in the Atlantic waters, trips to summer resorts, where he enjoyed the social pleasures to

*AS FULL BACK-1892.*

the utmost, stimulating victories in foot-ball, in which he made himself famous, an extension of acquaintanceship in all ports where duty called him, and a growing of his mental faculties and an enlargement of his views and sympathies. His letters to his mother, his sisters and his brothers were frequent and grew in number and in expressions of tender love. They are so full of affection, of noble sentiment, of patriotism, and give so clear an insight into his inner life that the task of selecting a few extracts from the many of the same tenor, so as to let his letters tell the story o his last four years at the Academy, has not been easy. It is believed that the extracts which follow will give to the reader a conception of a young man who was as tender and loving at home, as thoughtful and considerate of his comrades, and as generous and high-minded in peace as he was brave and fearless in the solemn hour of his tragic and heroic death.

Oct. 11th, '91: "I am so glad that you came in my room that day when I was showing you around here. Sometimes I think 'Well, mama has been in here', and it makes me feel real good and happy."

Nov. 8th, '91: "I was so sorry to hear about Judge Shepherd's son's death, but it should not be considered as a sorrowful death, dying as he did. If we could all die in that way, I would say 'let me die' and it would be a pleasure. Such faith and in such a young boy! It will surely lessen the sorrow of his family."

Dec. 13th, '91. "What do you think about my coming home? I was afraid you would think it too expensive for so short a stay, but I would be willing to work forever to go...... I just *must* go, I have been just wild for the last month to be at home and sit down in a nice, warm rocker by the fire with all the home folks around."

Dec. 22nd, '91: "I am so glad I can come home that I don't know what to do."

Jan. 17th, '92: "All the talk here now is war. We talk perpetually of that and nothing else. Everybody hopes that we will be ordered to sea in active service......I am afraid the fourth class will not get a chance, at least for two years, if the war lasts that long .....I am going to apply for permission to go as I am well up in seamanship, drill, &c. Just think how fine that would be....The Chilians depend most on a vessel of theirs now nearing completion in France which we cannot match; but I think we will declare war before she is completed and then declare an embargo on her which France cannot violate, as she is being built by Frenchmen in a French shipyard. A Chilian cruiser is being built in England also, and the same embargo will be declared in her case, too. Neither will be violated then, we may be sure, for England does not desire to pay $15,000,000 damages again as she did in the case of the Alabama in our late war. The fight will be even at the start or perhaps we may sustain a few losses, as Chilian soldiers are in training after their last war and very hot headed. They give no quarter and the throats of all their enemies left wounded on the field are ripped with knives made especially for that purpose. If they adopt this mode of warfare for their ordinary enemies, what can we Americans, whom they utterly detest, expect?...... There will hardly be any chances for our naval officers other than captains of vessels to distinguish themselves in the modern manner of warfare, and here the army have an advantage over us ........ Every one here is praying for war and it will help to remedy the present stagnation in promotion in our arm of the service."

Spring of 1892: (Writing of the visit of fifteen Austrian Naval Cadets to the Academy, telling how he had devoted the day as one of a committee to entertain them): "At the Austrian Academy they are allowed to drink and smoke as they choose. They were with us at dinner today. The cadet I was with told me rather bluntly that they were very much surprised that we had offered them nothing to drink at table. I thought that the nobleman's son was brought up rather badly to make such an impolite remark, and told him that we were not allowed anything to drink. 'Not allowed anything to drink!' he cried in French. 'Mon Dieu. I do pity you American Cadets!' I got rather angry at his 'pitying us American Cadets', so I said rather hotly 'Ne vous ennuyez, Monsieur, nous sommes tres bien contents.' (Don't bother yourself, we are very well contented.) He noticed how his remark had been taken and apologized; so after that we were very good friends........ We treated them very nicely and when they left us to go on board their steam launch (the vessel is three miles out) they all tossed their hats about their heads and hollered 'Au revoir.' We answered them and started to give the Academy yell, but remembering that they could not understand English, we were afraid they would think we were *hooting* at them."

April 17th, '92: "I would like to get some letters this week on Wednesday, Thursday, and Friday as they are our examination days..... That trip to California will be something simply fine for you, mama. You don't know how good it makes me feel for you to get a chance to go off and enjoy yourself. I will be a great deal happier than were I to take the trip and a thousand times more disappointed if you don't go than I would be were I to be cut out of such a trip. You just shall go."

May 1st, 92: "I was perfectly delighted with the flowers. They are in front of me on the table and give a delicious odor to the room. The banksias particularly remind me of home, as I can imagine the front porch covered with them."

May 1st, 92. "If I were a politician I would lay for sneaks and expose them."

June 10th, '92: "I starred for the year and stand 3rd in the class with a very good mark.... . Tell Addie I think the red stone is the prettier ..... I am so proud "starring," as much for the ring as the honor, but did not fully realize it until I saw the stars on my jacket at the June ball."

New London, Conn., July 11th, '92: "I have been very homesick for a week or more..... I really do not believe that any home in this world is as dear and loving as ours..... Kiss Adelaide and don't forget to teach her my name if she can learn it before I get home...... Thank God I was taught to despise vulgar language and habits when I was little."

Long Island Sound, July 19th, '92: "You would be perfectly in love with the Navy if you could see the ships of the North Atlantic squadron. Admiral Gherardi is in command of the fleet and the Philadelphia is his flag ship. I went aboard the Philadelphia and Miantonomoh Friday morning and enjoyed looking them over very much indeed. I was struck with the discipline and rigor with which the ship is run. Everything is done like clock work, especially on the flag ship. From stem to stern and from spar-deck to keel the ships themselves are neatness personified."

New London, July 31st. '92 : "I am not in favor of———'s going out of the State. We all have so many friends in North Carolina..... It would seem like leaving the whole world to me."

Jamestown, R. I. Aug 12th, '92 : "I am sure nobody in the world ever had a home like ours and how thankful we should be for it."

Annapolis, Oct. 3rd, '92 : "I feel mighty homesick and complain continually that I can't be back in my own dear little home. Mother, how much I love you and my dear brothers and sisters nobody in the world but myself knows. How I wish I could be home with you."

Nov. 3rd, '92: (To his sister Belle at school in Chambersburg, Pa) "I received a real nice long letter from mother to-day. It just breathed of home and home life and consequently I enjoyed it and haven't ceased to enjoy it. I shall read it again after awhile before going to bed."

Feb. 5th, '93. "My letters from home are ' chewed and digested ' as Carlyle has it..........I was delighted and had to take Adelaide's picture out and laugh all to myself to think that she is running about the house by herself. I think about her a great deal and love the picture I have of her. I am so glad I have it. I am sure it does me lots of good."

Oct. 22nd, '93: "This is Sunday afternoon and a very rainy, dreary one with the prospect of a hard, very hard, week ahead of me. This is exam. week..... I have worked myself up to a good old home-sick feeling this afternoon. I believe I love to get real home-sick in a room by myself, and have the rain patter against the panes as it does now, and have the wind whistle and moan through the cracks. I always feel that come what will, exams. or no exams., ' bilge ' or graduate, I have such a dear home that would be more than a recompense for it all. I think it is a sweet, cry-baby sort of feeling that we often love to indulge in."

Nov. 20th, '93 : "Please let me have lots of letters this week of ' exams.' "

Aug. 4th, '94: "I have been transferred from the Monongahela to the Bancroft with the rest of my class." In the same letter, writing of the birth of his nephew, "I want to tell you how happy I was to get the delightful news. It was so fine that I am tickled to death......I shall certainly bring the young naval officer a package of cigarettes to teethe with when I come on leave. That and a good bottle of Annheuser-Busch will start him well on the track of the Navy, which my heart is set on his entering. We have not had enough naval men in our family, and I want to offer the suggestion that he be given as a votive offering to his country's service in the navy. I will be there to look after him, that's the reason I want him. I shall make it my duty whether desired or not (?) to inculcate into him all possible seamanship knowledge and he shall be able to find the latitude and longitude of Raleigh or Washington by the time he is twelve years old. I think about him lots and am so anxious to see what he looks like..........I am glad of the good time you are having, but of all the good news the arrival of the young admiral has caused me the greatest happiness I have had in a long time."

Aug, 4th, '94 : "I am assistant Navigator now on the Bancroft.

The following letter, written a few days after the birth of his nephew, is printed in full because it is believed to give his high ideals of life and duty—ideals which he carried into the daily discharge of his duties: The letter was addressed, showing his playful humor, to

"COMMODORE JOSEPHUS DANIELS, JR.,":

ANNAPOLIS, MD.,
Sunday, Aug. 2nd, 1894.

MY DEAR YOUNG (?) NEPHEW—

I make an early reply to your letter announcing your most welcome arrival, in order to show my appreciation of the honor you have conferred upon me in allowing me to be the first to receive a letter from your hand.

Your handwriting is strangely like your father's: you will be lucky, sir, if you resemble him in other traits and qualities of heart or mind—I came within an ace of adding "looks," but I love you little one already, and shall wish you no such hard luck.

I shall help to bring you up in the right way when I am at home. Do not cry when I inform you that you must eat hard tack and salt horse from now on so that you may get used to the diet Worse yet you must have a copy of Luce's Seamanship right at hand even while sleeping and eating. Then on your first-class cruise you won't have the trials to undergo that your uncle is now passing through.

Above all, you must learn to be self-reliant. You must be a man at fifteen; it won't be hard for you to accomplish it. Never ask any favors if you can help it. Be a lady's man but don't tell each and all of them that you love them; at first some of them will believe you which will be sad for them, afterward none of them will believe you which will be sad for you.

Study hard and, until you enter the Naval Academy, don't pretend you know a thing until you do know it. Don't be a book worm or a hot house plant but take the proper exercise and make yourself a strong man. Don't tell a lie even at the Naval Academy. Love your father and mother and obey orders. It is as bad to disobey orders from the proper source as it is to tell a lie.

Keep this letter and I will keep yours, then someday we will compare. You will laugh then and wonder if your uncle kept all these things.

He didn't, that is the reason he wants to warn you beforehand and make an officer of you: you won't have the faults that he had.

But he will repeat to you what was said to him and the rest of the Navy team last year before the game with West Point which we won 6 to 4. Mind it wherever you may be. It is: "For God's sake keep your nerve, and show the stuff you're made of!"

With every good wish, and the hope that your young life begun in a bed of roses will suffer from only enough thorns to make a man of you in the time of danger and necessity, I am,

Your loving uncle,
WORTH BAGLEY.

Life ran along with him pleasantly, with no cloud on his horizon, until May, 1895, when there came like a clap of thunder out of a clear sky, from an unexpected quarter, a trouble that threatened his graduation. From his babyhood he had been physically perfect, and his fondness for athletics had developed his muscles until he was conscious of being capable of any amount of physical endurance. The following letter written home on May 5th, 1895, told of his trouble:

"I have learned from a good source that I am recommended to be dropped physically on account of my heart...... ...Last year on the annual physical examination the doctors found that the apex of my heart had shifted to the left about two inches, due to violent exercise. The right side had enlarged in muscle and had naturally forced the apex to the left. This is not at all dangerous and does not by any means affect a man's life or efficiency.........The doctors noted the fact on my record and held me over but advised me not to indulge in violent exercise then or the next fall at foot-ball without first consulting them. When the foot-ball season came around during the following fall I said I would not play and did not do so for about a month when every one begged me to come out......Some of the boys said I had the big head, and only wanted to be begged, etc., so I said if Doctor ——— would examine me and recommend me to play that I would do so. So he examined me and said that it would not hurt me at all. So I played. Since that time, last December, I have taken no violent exercise at all.........I am going to tell the Superintendent that I am not satisfied with the verdict and wish to have another examination, and ask permission to request it of the Secretary of the Navy. A cadet just graduating is worthy of such consideration ......... Dr.———, who examined me a year ago says I am fit for the service physically...... I hope you can come to Washington. It would be best for us to be in Washington at the same time..... I feel that I am all right physically, having never been in the slightest degree unable to perform such duties as ordinarily came my way......... I have heard that the Surgeon General is an able and a square man, and I believe if he could know how well and healthy I am, he would hold me over."

To his mother at the same time he wrote:

"I am pretty confident of getting held over for my two years cruise at the least, and of passing on my return as well for I am confident that nothing is the matter with me. I am going to make use of the fact that I have played foot-ball for years without ever feeling the slightest hurt to my heart ......... Keep up your spirits and I feel sure all will come out well."

The Secretary of the Navy granted a re-examination, and the Examining Board recommended that he be held over for the final examination at the end of the two years cruise and then to determine, in June, 1897, whether the enlargement of the heart was such a physical infirmity as to disqualify him for service in the Navy. This decision gave him great happiness for he felt confident that in two years time it would be demonstrated that his heart was as sound as a dollar.

Writing to his oldest brother May 30th, 1895, he gave this good counsel:

"Write and tell me all about school; it would be a great thing for you if you will realize like the sensible person you are, just exactly how real-

...ngs that they loved. A sweeter home scene, with the mother at the piano and this noble youth leading in the melody that filled the house and floated out on the summer evening air, could not be found anywhere. His love for music and his fine voice made him friends wherever he was called. The daughter of an Army officer, writing from Boston a few days ago, gives one of the many glimpses of the delights that his love of music brought to him and to others:

"At Old Point, where I saw him most, the men used to meet at our house a great deal and with a banjo, guitar and autoharp, would sing to while away the time. Worth often made one of our number and always added greatly to the singing. His voice, as you know, was extremely sweet. I remember that two of his favorite songs at that time were 'Don't you hear dem bells' and the 'Little Alabama Coon'. I can see him now leaning against the door and singing 'a Ringing out the Glory of the Navy' and 'Way down yonder in the corn field'. Generally we ended with 'God be with you till we meet again'—the men sang it so well."

His friends had his whole heart. One of the closest was Cassius Bartlett Barnes, son of Governor Barnes of Oklahoma. In a desire to render a service to this friend he wrote to a relative:

"You have heard me speak of Barnes, one of my best friends. I would do anything in the world I could for him, and many a time he has proved his friendship for me...... You have had men friends of the kind that one loves—he is one of these to me."

From Key West, June 1st, 1896, while he was on the ill-fated Maine, writing to his mother he said:

"Your letters are such dear ones. The last made me live over again that delightful day at Old Point which I will never forget......It is not near as hot here as one would expect, for nearly always there is a breeze from the sea."

His assignments in the Navy pleased him very much. Shortly after he first went on the Maine, he wrote to his mother:

"I believe you know that Breckinridge and I are rooming together now. (They had been room-mates at Annapolis most of the time when they were cadets and were like David and Jonathan in their friendship—EDITOR.) The Maine is a fine ship and we are very well satisfied this time."

Having twice served on the Texas, he always defended it from the criticisms of the press, feeling that it was an old friend. He was on the Texas in September, 1896, when it ran aground in New York harbor. Writing home he gave a graphic account of the accident.

The time had come, June 1897, to have the final test of his heart made to ascertain whether he could receive his commission.

TAKEN IN JANUARY. 894.

Dr. Warfield, president of Lafayette College, Easton, Pa., tells the result of the examination in an interview published on the 16th day of May, 1898:

"Ensign Bagley was a classmate and intimate friend of my cousin, Ensign Joseph Cabell Breckinridge, who was washed overboard from the Cushing near Havana a few months ago. I first met him at Washington. He had come up from Annapolis in great anxiety because the examining board had reported that he had heart trouble, brought on by football. He came to General Breckinridge in search of 'influence', but the General was absent on an inspecting tour, and the 'influence' was not forthcoming. I was very much struck by his frank and manly ways, and offered to see Assistant Secretary Roosevelt for him. We found the enthusiastic secretary most skeptical as to 'football heart', and a few minutes examination by a medical officer of high standing gave Mr. Bagley a clean bill of health, and the forthcoming certificate insured his promotion as Ensign. He was the happiest and most grateful fellow I ever saw. I have often heard his fellows at the Academy sing his praises. He was a famous back on the football team, and though very popular, as modest and as unassuming as a manly man always is. In every way he was the kind of a young man to whom we look to do the country credit. It is very strange that the two young men in whose promotion I was especially interested should thus be killed at the opening of the war."

As soon as he knew his commission would be issued he hastened with the good news to his home in Raleigh to gladden the heart of his mother and family. He was perfectly happy, feeling that all his troubles were past, and he was prouder to be an officer of the American Navy than any earthly honor or wealth could have made him, and in his joy, with forty days leave, he had made many plans for bringing happiness to his home-folks. He was welcomed with love and pride, and dreams of an ideal vacation were being realized when his mother became ill. In a few days the disease was pronounced appendicitis and her physician decided that an operation was necessary to save her life. In this hour, his fortitude and his tenderness upheld his brothers and sisters and gave comfort to his sick mother. He accompanied his oldest sister and family physician on the journey with his mother to Johns Hopkins Hospital, Baltimore, and it was his strong arms about her and his brave spirit that gave strength and comfort. Writing to his brother-in-law from the hospital, of the operation, he said .

"Mother did not make a murmur in regard to the knife. As a man, I feel vastly proud of her courage. When they came for her to take her to the operating room, I went into the room unknown to her to see that they didn't handle her roughly as they sometimes do, you know, * * As she passed me on the stretcher, she lifted her hand up for me to take, all the time looking out of her eyes with the same expression of resignation that the Savior is pictured with. * * We, (Addie and I) were informed that the operation would be over in fifteen minutes, and we waited thirty, we waited forty-five, and an hour. Then came a half-hour that neither of us will ever forget, for that stretcher didn't appear till one hour and a half had elapsed ! Toward the last, I felt as though a bomb were inside of me and that I was to be blown into a thousand pieces....Well, from the time the stretcher left the room till it returned we waited on the balcony outside of mother's window.......I remember turning around to look at Addie ; she was sobbing but otherwise apparently calm, and accused me of crying. Such nerve in a woman was too much for me, so I took a brace for very shame of it."

When his mother was well enough for him to leave, his orders for duty as an Ensign had come, and he went to duty thankful that in her serious illness, his vacation made it possible for him to render her every service that love and tenderness could prompt.

## CHAPTER IV.

### FULL BACK ON THE NAVY FOOT-BALL TEAM.

ALWAYS fond of sports requiring physical strength and daring, the young cadet soon became a leader in athletics at the Naval Academy. In the gymnasium and on the field he excelled. During his first term he was on his class base-ball team, and came to be one of the brag base-ball players at the Academy. He took part in the running and jumping and other contests in the department of athletics, and won four Naval Academy Auxiliary Athletic Association medals. But foot-ball was his athletic passion, and when he had become a champion in that most exciting and hazardous of games, other sports seemed tame to him. He became an authority on how to play the game.

In his second year at the Academy, was regarded among the cadets as one of the best foot-ball players. The following extracts from his letters home during that season, show his love of the game, his pride in his success, and the way he bore his injuries :

Nov. 23rd, '90 : "I made my debut as a half back yesterday afternoon in the game between the team and the Deaf and Dumb College, Kendall. As a consequence, I am laid up to-day with a sore leg and arm, nothing serious of course. But my playing was complimented so by the fellows that I did not mind my bruises much. I am now sitting in my warm room. the doctor's liniment on one hand, my photograph album on the other, and writing a letter home. I really feel delightful. Our team beat 24 to 0, and while we were in a very broken contition, too. Our really two best players were laid up in the hospital. We want them to get perfectly well before Thanksgiving day so they can play against our old friend, Lehigh, which was the only team that beat us last year. Our team leaves here the morning after Thanksgiving day and goes to West Point where they play Saturday afternoon. We are very anxious to beat West Point and Lehigh, as we have not been beaten yet this season, and only tied once."

Dec. 6th, '90: "When I got your letter last Thursday night, I nearly went wild over it. I read it I don't know how many times......My football last month didn't hurt me at all in my studies as you see from my report."

Dec. 7th, '90: "We have the satisfaction of knowing that we walloped West Point in the dust, 24 to 0, notwithstanding the excuses which the papers make for West Point..........I forgot to tell you that I am on the excused list again for foot-ball, not hurt bad enough to speak of, though my leg pains me slightly when I walk. I have the consolation of knowing, however, that I made the winning touch-down and goal for the class of '93 before I quit playing. I have some good liniment and am feeling finely up here in my room writing while all are at church, but it is rather cold to-day though and has been for a week or more."

He first played as quarter back and then as full back on the Annapolis team. He kept a scrap book which he called "Notes in Athletics" in which he preserved all the newspaper accounts of the notable games, and recorded the names of the foot-ball and base-ball teams at the Academy. His absorbing interest in the contest between the army and navy is shown by the fact that on the first page of his scrap book in his clear round hand this record appears:

SCORES IN CHAMPIONSHIP SERIES.
ANNAPOLIS AND WEST POINT.

1890—Annapolis, 24; West Point, 0.
1891—Annapolis, 16; West Point, 32.
1892—Annapolis, 12; West Point, 4.
1893—Annapolis, 6; West Point, 4.

In his "Notes on Athletics," this extract is copied from F. Marion Crawford: "Brave natures—good and bad alike—hate falsehood not for its Wickedness, perhaps, but its Cowardice."

His pride in being chosen on the team to play West Point in 1891 is seen in an extract from a glowing letter written to his youngest sister on the 4th of November of that year. He wrote:

'I am on the foot-ball team this year. At the beginning of the season we had Poe, who used to be captain of the Princeton team, here to coach our team and to decide who was to belong to it. He had the team to play against the second team before him so he could see how we played. From that he was to choose the team. Just think! I brought myself under the notice of the immortal Poe himself and he recommended me for quarter back on the Naval Academy eleven! His recommendation was the same as my election. So I am and have been all this season on the foot-ball team. We have played two games so far, one against St. John and one against Rutger's College. We beat St. John 28 to 6 and Rutger's 21 to 12. I have played well enough in both games to get myself especially mentioned in the New York World, Sunday, for the last two weeks. The Baltimore American and the Annapolis papers mentioned me very flatteringly, too. Our team this year is considered one of the finest in America and we are very proud of it. I am the lightest man on it and weigh 151."

Before the game of 1891, his letters home were full of references to it, all of them indicating that he thought the result in doubt. On the 8th of November he wrote:

"Everybody is looking forward to our game with West Point at the close of the season, Saturday after Thanksgiving. West Point is confident. They have written articles to the World about how badly they are going to beat us, etc...... The Naval Academy keeps silent wisely; does not seek to bluff by newspaper articles and is certainly not bluffed in return. We simply wait for the game which will decide the contest better......If we get beat New Quarters will be draped in mourning. Everybody is assured of one fact, however, and that is that West Point will beat us only after the hardest tussle they ever had. The team is composed of older and heavier men than ours, but we have the muscle, and the grit and spirit of younger men."

Writing on the 15th of November he said:

"We have had two foot-ball matches since I wrote you last Sunday. One was on Wednesday when we played the team from Georgetown University (Washington), and defeated them 16 to 4. I made a touch down in this game, the first made during the game. Then we played a game with Dickenson College, one of the strong teams North, and beat them 34 to 4. I made two touch downs, one after a run of 75 yards; the other, after a run of 40 yards. I don't suppose you will see the Sunday Herald, so I will tell you what it said about my first touch down of 75 yards. The article was headed 'Middies vs. Theologians' and it gave a short account of the game. One of the things it said was: 'Within two minutes after the beginning of the second half, Bagley, the cadet quarter-back, made a brilliant run of over two-thirds of the length of the field (seventy-five yards), dodging through Dickenson's line and scoring a touch down.' I have to keep in training all the time and it is no easy work either, I can tell you ...I have not been hurt at all except yesterday, I bit just a little piece out of my lip. My nose (usually so small?) is now shaped like the side of a bracket. It is not hurt, though, and I can still smell and breathe through it with ease.'

When West Point won by 32 to 16, his letters home show how he took defeat. Nov. 30, 1891:

"We are beaten as you have already read no doubt in the New York papers. The score was 32 to 16 ..... They were all large men, averaging nine pounds more than ours.... I did not write yesterday, I was suffering from a slightly sore back which is nearly well, however, to-day. I wish I could be home. I just feel awfully homesick lately. The West Point game didn't take away any of the feeling either, I can tell you..... One of the songs sung on the foot-ball field by the cadets was to the tune of 'Marching Through Georgia.' The chorus is all I remember:

"We'll rush, we'll rush, we'll rush the ball along,
We'll rush, we'll rush, we'll rush it through the throng,
With Macklin running round the end
And Bagley by his side,
Working like the devil for a touch down."

Dec. 6th, '91 : " I could not help showing my disappointment over the game with West Point, and one of the officers patted me on the shoulder and said : 'Brace up, old man, we'll beat them next year when we get our coaches. We are still ahead because we beat them last year 24 to 0.' I replied, 'Yes, sir, but if I had only gotten my leg broken or something like that during the game, I would feel more consolation'. He laughed and went on. Several spoke to me in the same manner..... I wouldn't have missed playing in that game for a good round sum, even if we did get beat. The game was grand. At one time both teams were striped with blood, but still we fought like two dying game cocks to the bitter end and *I felt exactly as I imagine I would feel in battle, threatened with defeat and carried away with excitement. Not a thought of danger entered my head*, and if it did I would be ashamed to own it. It was not a 'fighting' game, but both teams strove so hard that eight men were carried off the field wounded. I did my best during the game and had the satisfaction of hearing many times a yell composed especially for my name."

The New York World of Nov. 14th, 1891, said :

"Bagley, quarter back, is a beautiful sprinter. His drop and punt kicks are fine, and he is a most valuable man. He is light, weighing 148 pounds."

Writing of the Thanksgiving game when West Point won, the New York Times said :

"Davidson advanced over the ground like a shot from a gun. Bagley alone stood between him and the goal. Would Bagley stop him? He would."

This closed his first season as a member of the Annapolis team. Instead of being dismayed by defeat, it nerved him for more thorough training in order to be ready for the 1892 game. Writing on the 13th of December he said :

"I will probably play full back next year instead of quarter back, and that is the most responsible position, except being captain of course. It is hard to say whether we will beat West Point, but every effort will be used to accomplish that end."

He always believed a naval cadet was better trained than a cadet at West Point, and therefore, in spite of difference in age or weight, could win in a trial of strength. The record of the foot-ball contests confirmed his faith. In the Spring and Summer of 1892, before the foot-ball season opened, he took part in the athletic contests. On June 10th, he wrote to his mother:

"Saturday before annual week, the Spring athletic sports were held at the Academy, all entries open to cadets only. I won medal for the half mile run, making the half mile in 1 minute and 58 4-5 seconds. The medal is a silver one about the size of a dollar. The badge to which it is attached is in the shape of a shield and is silk of Academy colors, navy blue and gold. I have the medal in my trunk and will bring it home when I go on leave."

His ambition was realized and when the team was announced for 1892, he was promoted to full back. The following extracts from his letters show his elation of spirit:

"Oct. 16th. '92: "Don't tell anybody, but several of the papers after this game said that I was 'undoubtedly the most valuable man on the team.'"

"Nov. 20th, '92: "I am thankful that the foot-ball season will soon be over. It will be over for us next Saturday after the West Point game... We played Georgetown University yesterday and beat them 40 to 0. I made four touch downs and kicked three goals from touch downs, making 22 of the 40 points....I am so glad I am going to West Point next week, and I will go unless I get hurt in a practice game tomorrow or day after....Both teams have very fine records so far this season and a very close game may be expected. I shall be very much disappointed if we don't win, but we have a very heavy and a very well coached team to play against us......I can't think of anything but that game, and often I dream about it. If we win, we will be kings here at the Academy; if we lose, we will feel very bad....I wish my little mama was going to watch me play next Saturday."

Nov. 30th, '92: (To his oldest brother) "I have about risen to the zenith of my glory, I guess, having been especially mentioned in Harper's Weekly. The sporting editor of that paper is very careful about complimenting, too ...Since the game with Pennsylvania our team has improved wonderfully. We held Princeton down to the smallest score she has made this year. Pennsylvania beat us 18 to 0, but since then we have beaten LaFayette 22 to 4, and several days after the game Pennsylvania only beat them 8 to 6. ..I made a touch down from centre of field without any interference for me at all......We have the best team the Navy has ever produced .....My hair is nearly four inches long and I plaster it down on my head until games. It protects my head from the hard ground."

His joy when the Annapolis team won over the West Pointers in the Thanksgiving game of 1892 at West Point by a score of 12 to 4 knew no bounds. He wrote of his happiness with the fresh ardor of victorious youth, and sent the New York papers home so that his home folks might read the minutest details of the game.

A song, the "Middies' Revenge" written of this game, to the tune of "Boom de ay", made this reference to him:

> "Rushing like a mighty blizzard,
> Thro' the lines flew little 'Izard',
> And when 'Bagley' kicked the 'goal',
> Terror seized on every soul."

Of this game Casper W. Whitney, in Harper's Weekly, said: "Bagley punted with much judgment." The New York Times' account of the game said: "Then more wedges, till the ball was put over the West Point line for another touch down by Bagley, and the same man kicked the goal." The New York Morning Advertiser said: "Bagley kicked the goal. The enthusiasm of the Naval boys knew no bounds at this juncture." The Annapolis Capital said:

"Everybody climbed up on chairs to see the attempt at goal and when Bagley sent the ball high above and directly between the goal posts, a demonstration followed which would have satisfied a newly elected president......Back to Bagley went the ball and into the line he went and another touch down was the result."

A paper showing some records made by naval cadets for the year '92-3, contain the following reference: "4 goals, Bagley, '95 (from 30 yard line—5 kicks allowed.)" In his score of the season, in seven games, he writes "opponements 64 : U. S. N. A. 146."

The eyes of all lovers of foot-ball in America turned to the game of 1893, played at Annapolis, between the navy and the army teams. Full back Bagley was confident of victory and played with such skill and genius as to win world-wide reputation in foot-ball circles. He had the joy of victory, for the score was 6 to 4 in favor of the Naval Academy team. The papers were full of the praise of the navy team and they all gave Bagley the credit of winning the game. The high officers of the Navy were as proud of the young Carolinian's prowess as the most enthusiastic "plebe" at the Academy. A trophy of this game was a gold foot-ball, made by Tiffany, to be used as a watch charm, on which was engraved: "Worth Bagley, Full-back, 1893."

The following is the first verse of a song "The Team That Won the Victory for the Navy," to the air "The Man that Broke the Bank at Monte Carlo", that the cadets sung in honor of the victory:

> "Oh we've just done up the Army,
> And they are feeling pretty sore
> For you should have heard us roar
> When we shoved the pigskin o'er;
> And when Bagley kicked the goal,
> Why, we shouted all the more,
> And when time was called we had them, six to four,
> Yes when time was called we had them, six to four."

"How Bagley Won the Game" is the subject of an article that recently appeared in the New York Evangelist. It is a more concise account than any that appeared at the time and is given place here:

"Although the war has thus far been almost bloodless, there has been at least the sacrifice of one precious life that is a great loss—that of Ensign Bagley, the first of our brave officers to fall. The death of one so young and so full of life recalls a gay scene at the navy yard at Annapolis in November, 1893, where he for the first time appeared as a hero. It was the day of the great foot-ball game between the army and the navy. A fine team of athletic young West Pointers had come down for a trial of strength with the naval cadets, and the friendly contest had drawn the crowds of army and navy men and of gay women, young and old, wearing the colors of the two branches of the service, and full of enthusiasm for the rival combatants.

"As the stalwart West Pointers appeared on the field they seemed so much larger and heavier than the Annapolis team that experts declared there would be an easy victory for the visitors, and the groups of army friends were correspondingly triumphant, but as the game began it was evident that the conflict would be a hard fought one, and as one good stand after another was taken by the slight, blue-uniformed boys, interest increased on both sides. There was a genuine admiration and satisfaction in the tones of the gray-haired navy surgeon as he rose to his feet and cheered at a good stroke, declaring, 'Our boys may be small, but they have got sand.'

"Finally, at a very critical moment, a slight figure emerged from the mass of struggling men and, seizing his opportunity, gave the hard-fought ball a kick that sent it far above the heads of all contestants to the other end of the gridiron and scored a much-needed point for the navy that saved the game.

"Only those who have watched such a contest can understand the enthusiasm of the scene; how hats went into the air and the name of Bagley was sounded with cheers from one end of the ground to the other.

"In the midst of all the enthusiasm a quiet little woman had arrived alone, and after vainly trying to find the seat reserved for her, caught the name that was on every one's lips and, turning with a flushed face to her neighbor in the crowd, said: 'Oh, I wish I could see what it is, for that is my son, and I have just arrived from North Carolina.' A place was speedily made for the proud little mother, and she watched her boy's triumph and saw him at the end of the game carried off the field on the shoulders of his mates amid the most resounding cheers. Foot-ball men declared his 'punt' had broken the record, and Bagley was the hero of the hour.

FOOT-BALL TEAM OF 1893.
(BAGLEY SITTING ON EXTREME RIGHT, NO. 5)

"From that day to this the mother's pride has never known a check; the boy successfully finished his course at the Academy holding the respect of his comrades and of his superior officers until the moment when he gave his fresh young life for his country on the deck of the Winslow. The broken-hearted mother has the consolation of knowing that many hearts all over our broad land are honoring her dead and sorrowing with her."

In a letter to his youngest brother written in 1895, he tells how a boy should learn to punt:

"Mother wrote me that she gave you a real foot-ball for Christmas. I am so glad and hope you will learn how to kick well. When you punt, drop the ball, bend forward slightly and kick it with the lower part of your instep with a hard side swing of your leg. Measure your punts and by practice you will improve. The longest I ever made without wind was sixty yards. Learn to drop the ball with the point down, not crooked. To kick a drop kick, let the ball fall almost vertically and directly on the end. Then kick forward hard, and strike the ball as it hits the ground. The bottom of your foot should almost scrape the ground when in the act of kicking, so your toe will strike the ball near the ground. To kick a place kick for goal, stand the ball vertically on end, and get opposite seams in a line with the goal. Take four or five steps toward it and kick with all your might, striking the ball about an inch and a half from the ground."

The daughter of an army officer, in whose home Ensign Bagley was a favorite guest, writes of one of the last games of football he played:

"I remember one day at Fort Monroe the Army men and Navy men were to play a game of foot-ball. I had never been able to see Annapolis and West Point, so was most anxious to see this game. I remember also that father at the beginning was much opposed to the game, but when it was over I think he was the most enthusiastic man in the post. Worth was playing and of course we expected him to do wonders as usual. Some of the men, however, thought he might have lost his knack, not having played for so long a time, but he showed them he had not by kicking a beautiful goal from the field, thus winning the day for them. The whole place went wild, and officers, old and young, in both Army and Navy could not say enough in his praise."

The Portland (Maine) Press says that Ensign Bagley had visited that port several times, and left many friends behind him when his ship sailed. The writer evidently knew him well and was well posted on his foot-ball record, for he writes:

"Bagley and Breckenridge were the two most popular men of the class of '95. Bagley, with his handsome face and genial manners, was always surrounded by a crowd of cadets when their duties would allow it, and among the ladies he was by all odds the most popular. Besides being a good student and a good fellow, Bagley was a star foot-ball player. He played in three games with the West Point team, each time as full back, and each time he so distinguished himself that the New York and Baltimore papers could not say too much of his dashing, clever work. Mr. Whitney, of Harper's Weekly, complimented Mr.

Bagley by placing him as full back on the "All Star America" team, and that was indeed a great compliment when it is understood that the best foot-ball players from all the American colleges were selected for this team "on paper" because of their ability in their particular position.

"It was a great sight to see Bagley go into a game, for his skill was so great and his pluck so good that no matter how badly things were going for the "middies" Bagley always wore a smile and seemed to be the coolest man in the lot. The cadets ranged along one side of the field would open the game by giving the academy yell, and then followed their own special yell of admiration and encouragement for Bagley. He had failed on the academy examination in chemistry once, all because he could not classify certain substances which were soluble and insoluble. This was where the Bagley yell came from. It went something like this:

"Sol, sol insol sol,
Insol, insol sol,
Bagley."

"And how this yell used to roll out from the 50 cadets as the Naval Academy team came trotting out on to the field in their dirty foot-ball clothes and with their long hair waving in the breeze. And Bagley was the king of them all, the man who was never known to lose his head, and who was as sure on a punt or a catch as any man who ever chased the pigskin. Again and again he saved the Naval Academy team from defeat, and his wonderful courage and dash will not soon be forgotten by those who knew him.

"There are many pleasant stories the Naval Academy men have to tell of the 'Worthless' Bagley, as he was called by those most intimate with him. He roomed during the four years course at the academy with Breckinridge, who was drowned on another torpedo boat, the Cushing, while trying to get into Havana before the Maine affair. Bagley and Breckinridge were never left much to themselves, for to their rooms crowded the cadets at all hours for advice, for skylarking, for sympathy, for assistance in their studies, and many other things. And no one, not even a homesick plebe, entered this room that he did not come away feeling happier and more contented with his lot, for, though he might be hazed at d 'run' a little by Breckinridge and Bagley, he was never ill-treated or made unhappy by their treatment of him.

"And there was another one, the first young officer in the Navy to be killed by Spanish treachery, and that was D. R. Merritt. He, too, was a classmate of Breckinridge and Bagley, and a close and intimate friend of both of these fine fellows. Merritt was killed in the explosion of the Maine a few weeks after Breckinridge's death on the Cushing. These three men, Breckinridge, Bagley and Merritt, all classmates, all friends, and all remarkably fine young officers, will not soon be forgotten by their associates, and if the Young Ensigns and Assistant Engineers in the Navy who were classmates of these fine fellows ever get within gunshot of a Spaniard and don't more than square accounts with them for the death of these men it will be passing strange."

Among the letters received by the mother, many have been from the lovers of foot-ball. Robert Burns Wilson, in a sweet and tender note accompanying a poem with which this chapter is concluded, said:

"I with millions of others deeply sympathize with you and would be glad to be able to speak some word of cheer or comfort. Every mother's heart goes out to you in purest love and sorrow. I met your dear boy at Annapolis once..... I should be glad to know that this tribute may please the mother of so noble a soul. He is with the immortals." The poem is appended:

### BAGLEY AND FOUR AT CARDENAS BAY.

Five thousand for the five!
That is the call—that's the price they'll pay,
For the brave boys lost at Cardenas bay.
Five thousand for the five!
The brave Carolina lad was there.
Too eager for fight—too willing to dare,
He was there in the midst of the fray;
And he won his place in the warrior's heaven.
Bagley—"full back" of the old eleven,
O! many a score he made,
While the "gridiron" rang with deep, hoarse cries,
Till the echoes came back from Annapolis bay,
And he was the pride of a thousand eyes,
He that is dead to-day;
By God! it was good for the soul
To see the rout—to hear the shout—
When Bagley "scored a goal."

But it's over. The green gridiron game,
Though rough and fierce, was mild and tame
Compared with the crashing and roaring hell
Of the withering battle where Bagley fell,
But Bagley was still the same.
Careful and cool in the midst of alarm,
As though with a pigskin under his arm,
He fought for a last touch down. Alas!
'Tis the iron deck, not the soft, green grass,
And now in a losing game he played;
But his is the hero's soul.
True to the end of the fight he stayed,
He and the four brave lads at his side,
He and the four brave boys that died
In the fight at Cardenas bay;
Firm-footed and dauntless and unafraid;
And the boys will see that the price is paid,
For the guns are ready and grim.
Five thousand for the five—
That is the call, and Spain will pay
Theirs is the place in the warrior's heaven.
Bagley, "full back" of the old "eleven,"
And the men that fell with him.

Silence on board when they call the roll,
" Bagley and four at Cardenas bay."
Absent, but only in name.
Theirs is a place in the warrior's heaven,
Bagley—"full back" of the old eleven.
And four brave lads that fell with him.
Five names, the first of the roll—
In the battle's red flame, in the last great game,
At the finish, death "scored a goal."
Let the guns be ready and grim.
Five thousand for the five!
To be paid and without delay.

## CHAPTER V.

### AS ENSIGN IN THE NAVY.

WORTH BAGLEY was at the hospital with his convalescent mother when he received his commission as Ensign in the Navy, dated July 1st, 1897, and signed by the President and the Secretary of the Navy. He was ordered to report to the Indiana on the 10th of July. With a glad and thankful heart that he had been with his mother in her critical illness, he bade her good-bye and began his career as Ensign on the Indiana. On the 17th of August, he was transferred to the Maine, remaining on that ill-fated vessel as executive clerk to Capt. Sigsbee until November 19th of the same year when he was ordered to the Columbian Iron Works, Baltimore, as inspector, in connection with fitting out the torpedo boat Winslow. Of his short career before he went on board the Winslow there is little to be said except that he was a faithful and popular officer, winning the confidence and regard of his superior officers and the respect and admiration of those who served under him. Many expressions have come from officers and sailors, all agreeing that the Navy had no manlier officer or one who gave greater promise of useful and honorable service.

There was in his nature the innate spirit of the charming host, and it was his custom to invite his friends aboard ship to dinner or to luncheon. Here is a description of such an occasion described by a gentleman writing from Elizabeth, N. J.

"While the squadron was at Bar Harbor last summer, my youngest daughter and myself met your son among others of the young officers ...They naturally desired us to see their pet ship, so on a day appointed we went aboard. It was lunch time before we had gone over the vessel and the young gentlemen insisted upon our lunching with them, and also my daughter, who is only 18, sitting at the head of the table and presiding. It was a very jolly lunch, your son making himself especially agreeable and entertaining, and in that way, dispensing as it were, the hospitality of his own house."

He was much at Norfolk after he was commissioned Ensign and was a great favorite. The daughter of an army officer gives this view of him that shows one of his ways of having fun and giving pleasure:

"We used to turn the three rear rooms in our house over to our Navy friends to occupy whenever they liked. Mother called them her 'boys' and Worth was one of them. He used to take the greatest delight in dressing up in whatever he could find and acting for our amusement. He was full of fun and always so dignified in whatever he did. It was the greatest pleasure to have him around. When he would have us aboard ship he was delightful, and at a dance he was always a 'star.' .....It is indeed wonderful how perfect he was in so many things."

Commodore Geer, of the Maryland Naval Reserves, says:

"I knew poor Bagley well. We were shipmates together on the ill-fated Maine for nearly three weeks, when I was cruising in that ship undergoing instruction. He was a boyish-looking fellow, but as intrepid as a lion. He was proud of his uniform and of his profession and no one loved the Stars and Stripes better than he. His disposition was as sunny as ever man had, and he was beloved by the officers and men. While he was at the Naval Academy he was a leading football-player, in which game he excelled. He was very fond of a joke and many a pleasant hour have I spent in his company listening to his jolly yarns."

Corporal W. L. Byrnes, at Camp Collier at Lexington, Ky., says:

"I served under Ensign Bagley, having enlisted in the Navy when I was sixteen years of age. He was the first person to teach me the use of a gun after my first enlistment. He was the most popular officer among his subordinates I ever had any connection with. While never losing his sense of discipline, he was always dignifiedly polite to men under him, and was never a user of harsh or profane language."

The New York World, of May 12th, says:

"A naval officer under whom Ensign Bagley served said to-day that the Ensign was one of the most lovable young men in the navy."

When Lieut. Bernadou knew that he was to be given command of the Winslow he enquired from a number of junior officers whom of their grade they considered fittest to serve on a torpedo boat. Of five or six lists of many names thus formed, including that submitted by the late Ensign Breckinridge, Bagley's name was universally given first or second place. Deciding to offer Ensign Bagley the position, Lieut. Bernadou wrote him the following letter:

NEWPORT, R. I., August 19th, 1897.

DEAR MR. BAGLEY:

I have received preparatory orders to the torpedo boat Winslow and desire to choose my lieutenant. I am told that you are a good foot-ball player. Deeming that such ability represents a round of qualities necessary to an efficient torpedo boat officer, I write to ask you whether you desire to come to the Winslow. If you do, notify me on receipt of this letter....Upon hearing from you I will endorse your application to the Chief of the Bureau.

Yours truly,
JOHN B. BERNADOU.

To the letter a reply was made expressing some hesitation about acceptance, and adding that if the offer had been made a month later it would have been agreeable. Lieut. Bernadou replied that he would defer making the application "until the Winslow's trial approaches" and adding "if however you do not desire to come, please write me, and I will consider the incident as closed, and endeavor to select my second elsewhere." From a letter written to him by Lieut. Bernadou on the 10th of September, these extracts are taken:

'I am well pleased that you have decided to come to the Winslow. ....It is the manifest duty of every officer to look to his best professional interests; this is the explanation of Captain Sigsbee's contemplated action and your own; nor can he blame you for desiring to exchange to a torpedo boat from duty as his clerk. Again, it may be more of a compliment to have him endorse your orders unfavorably than favorably, in the present issue, as it is easy to understand why he does not wish to part with you."

From this letter it is seen that Capt. Sigsbee hated to part with his clerk, and that the young Ensign hesitated about leaving the Maine, to which and to whose captain he was warmly attached. In the light of the destruction of the Maine and the engagement of the Winslow at Cardenas, the debate in Ensign Bagley's mind, prior to his leaving the Maine for service on the Winslow, assumes the aspect of a choice between disasters. There is another incident connected with the change from the Maine to the Winslow that has a mournful interest. After Ensign Bagley had been offered the position of second in command on the Winslow and was hesitating about accepting, there came a long letter to him from his closest friend and intimate, Ensign J. Cabell Breckinridge, who had lately been made executive officer on the torpedo boat "Cushing", urging him not to stand in his own light by declining the proferred promotion, and closing with these words:

"You cannot imagine my disappointment when I heard that you were about to decide to remain a quill-driver when the opportunity of getting a torpedo boat, of getting with Bernadou (our smokeless powder expert and a man of numberless good qualities), and of putting yourself in line of succession to command, had been offered you

Ensigns will command torpedo boats before we are promoted and the men who get them will be men who have had previous experience.'

On the 12th day of February, this gallant young officer, whose advice may have turned the scale and induced Ensign Bagley to go to the Winslow, was washed overboard in the harbor of Havana from the torpedo boat Cushing. His death was the sorrow of Ensign Bagley's life. Writing to his mother a few days later, he said:

"Just a line to tell you that I leave here for Lexington via Washington to-night. General Breckinridge telegraphed me to come on. I am heart-broken. Thank you for your sweet sympathy. I shall ask the honor of commanding the volley over his dear body."

How little we then thought that in three short months the North Carolina volunteers would fire a volley "over his dear body", and that Worth Bagley would follow his friend to a deathless grave. In life they were not separated. In death they are not divided. When the boxes containing the letters, photographs, and valuables, of Ensign Bagley reached Raleigh after his death, side by side with the pictures of his mother and sisters were two photographs of Cabell Breckinridge, wrapped in crape, mutely telling the grief he felt at the sudden death of his room-mate, classmate, comrade, friend.

The following is the extract from his letter home announcing his transfer to the Winslow:

Nov. 27th, '97: (Written from Baltimore): "My present ambitions have been realized and I am in Baltimore on shore duty at Columbian Iron Works in connection with the torpedo boat 'Winslow', of which I am to be executive officer when she goes in commission in a few weeks, Lieutenant Bernadou commands her, and we will be the only officers on board. I will write you all about it. My orders raise me professionally, so I know you will be glad about them."

It was on the 28th of December when the Winslow went into commission and Ensign Bagley entered upon his duties as executive officer. He was proud of the little boat, came to have the warmest regard for Lieut. Bernadou, and to enjoy the confidence and esteem of the entire crew. In January last the young Ensign had opportunity to demonstrate that he had taken the advice he commended to his nephew "For God's sake keep your nerve, and show the stuff you are made of." In a raging storm, with the assistance of two sailors in a life boat, he saved the lives of two poor fellows from a scow which was adrift at sea about fifty miles from New York. For this deed, the Secretary of the Navy, on February 1st, wrote a letter of thanks to Lieut. Bernadou, Ensign Worth Bagley and the other members of the crew, closing with the words: "The service performed by the Winslow is not only gratifying to all who engaged in it but tends to reflect additional lustre upon the whole service."

Upon the arrival of the Winslow at Norfolk, after this narrow escape, it was necessary to make some repairs to the boat, and, while these were being made, Ensign Bagley obtained five days leave and spent from Tuesday to Saturday at his home in Raleigh. His home coming was always like the coming of Spring, bringing warmth and cheer and happiness. This time he was received as one who had narrowly escaped a watery grave. It was five days of such happiness as those who survive will ever look back upon as the sweetest period life has vouchsafed. He told the story of the adventure in the storm on the Jersey coast, only when his mother asked for the details, as if he had done nothing worthy of honor, but did not disguise the extreme peril of the situation.

He recounted the bravery of the crew and said that they bore themselves like courageous and noble men.

"On watch one night when the wind was blowing a gale, mother," he said, "and the weather was as cold as it could be, I found myself singing in an undertone, 'Anchored.'"

"Safe, safe at last,
The danger past,
Safe in his father's home,"

and—it seemed to give me hope and strength." The last words of that song which had strengthened him in the hour of peril were sung over his grave on the day of the funeral.

There was then talk of war with Spain. He believed in the righteousness of our cause and was eager for war. His mother, even at that time when war was not imminent, felt a sinking of the heart at the mention of it, and he sought to cheer her by telling her that it would be a short war and that if occasion offered he would distinguish himself. She believed that his courage and daring would carry him into places "where the bravest love to die," and had a premonition that his immortality would come at the sacrifice of his life. On Saturday, February 5th, for the last time he said good-bye to his home-folks, and went away to duty and to

BASE-BALL TEAM—1895.
(BAGLEY WITH BAT IN HAND ON THE LEFT.)

death. His mother clung to him with a yearning, a fondness, a caressing love that was born of her premonition of danger. His farewell was full of tender chivalry,

> "The bravest are the tenderest.
> The loving are the daring."

When the Maine was blown up in the harbor of Havana his righteous wrath was kindled into a blaze, and his letters were full of the spirit of war which dominated him. He wrote often and fully, and these letters show his faith in his country's cause and his eagerness for the fray. When his ship left Norfolk, he telegraphed his mother, and telegraphed her afterwards when it reached Charleston and Key West, hoping to minimize her anxiety by accurate knowledge of his movements.

Noting the presence of the Winslow at Charleston in March, the News and Courier said:

> "Ensign Worth Bagley, the executive officer of the Winslow, has visited Charleston before and has numbers of friends among both fair and gallant Charlestonians. He will be remembered also by many for his excellent work on the "gridiron" in a recent football game, "Uncle Sam" vs. the Y. M. C. A."

Hon. F. A. Woodard and wife, of Wilson, were at Key West about the 20th of March, and dined with him on the Winslow. Writing to Ensign Bagley's sister, Mr. Woodard said:

> "We were delighted to meet Worth. He is here and will leave in a few days. We went to see him at his ship and had a very pleasant talk with him and went over the boat. It is certainly a most interesting craft Lt. Bernadou is very pleasant and I was gratified to hear him speak so highly of Worth. He said he was one of the most promising of the young men of the Navy. Worth is looking splendidly."

By these friends he sent loving messages home, asking them to assure his mother that he was in no danger, was at the post of duty, and was chiefly anxious because of her anxiety.

His letters from March 3rd to May 8th, tell the story not only of the last two months of his life, but show also the nobleness of his nature, his thoughtfulness, his affection, his devotion, to "My Dearest Little Mother," as he began his last letter, his brave spirit, and the true faith of the soldier that was in him. These extracts are given:

March 3rd, '98: (Writing from Portsmouth): "We are on the eve of sailing and would have sailed this afternoon but for a telegram announcing a storm off the coast to-night. We will lay by till a favorable opportunity offers for a straight away run for Charleston. It will take us a little over a day to reach there, and we remain there long enough to fill up with coal. Then we proceed to Jacksonville in the same way, taking a long run then for Key West, our destination. I am very well......You will have to get out of the habit of feeling fear for my safety. I am always safe......Besides you have enough of the Spartan in you, if you wish, to say 'with your shield or on it' and that is what you must always say to me to give me strength and determination. You may be sure that I am not ashamed to use the proper amount of care of myself, and will think of you in the midst of every danger. These latter are few, after all; really there are none. ......I wish I could talk to you, for I have a great deal to tell you...... It must be pleasant to have every one well now. It makes me more contented about leaving....The next time we come to Norfolk, you are to come and make me a visit, and I'll return it if I can."

April 3rd, '98: (Written from torpedo boat Winslow): "It looks as though we are to have war; our work is for that reason even harder than usual, so that all hands on board the Winslow are thoroughly fatigued. I was never stronger or in better health in my life, but am tired nearly all the time. Often when needing sleep I find it much more refreshing to go ashore for the relaxation from confining work. These opportunities to get relaxation are, however, very few in number. I believe I am making a success of this work; at all events, Bernadou says nice things to everybody about me. This may be on account of a personal interest in my future, however, so I am by no means satisfied, for it is very apparent to me that there are innumerable things that should be familiar to me that I do not know. Bernadou is gaining confidence in me I hope, and leaves a great deal to me; he is very patient with me..... He is one of the most broad-minded men I have ever known, and one of the most far-sighted. He is certainly kind to me... You can readily see that, now that war is imminent, the torpedo boats have the best chances of distinction. Consequently we are envied right and left, by all young officers at least. You will of course be glad that my post, though one of danger, will be the most honorable. You may be well sure that I shall think of your dear face and see it before me whenever I am under fire, and if I get the opportunity to do some distinguished service you may know that the thought of the happiness it will give you is alone sufficient to make me seize it .....Do not fear that I shall be afraid, mother, but always remember that I have a certain amount of skill and strength wherewith to attack; don't think of me as in danger defending myself against a black-haired Spaniard with an ugly face, but think of me as blowing up the Dago lepers. The Spaniards will be easy prey for our Navy, which is in the most efficient condition. ... If the Spaniards back down now, it would be the source of the very bitterest disappointment. They will have to kneel and crawl in a manner that history has never before seen ...Why did they blow up our Maine? No matter what pretext any or all the members of Congress can give for war, *we must have it.* The cause of war lies in a set of American colors blown up in an explosion, and with the colors the men who served to protect them; blown up at night while asleep —evidence in itself sufficient to show that a contemptible Spaniard did it The blood almost fills my head when I think of this; it makes me almost wild with anger......I shall write you another letter soon, certainly before any fighting takes place. There is no great danger of my being killed, but should such a thing happen, there is not a great deal for me to say. You know how much I love you, dearest, don't you? Love to each one at home."

April 14th, '98: (Written from torpedo boat Winslow): "You must not fret about me. In the first place, there may be no war; this is very probable, I am afraid. In the second place, a Spaniard couldn't hit an honest American at pistol range; the Dago is too much a coward for that. The war, if it comes, will be very easy. The adversary is too poor an adversary for much glory to be gained for our flag. But it is to be hoped that we may sink some of their ships in return for the poor Maine. Do not be uneasy about me. I will not run into any danger I do not think proper, but can't promise you anything else; don't you know what I mean, dear? Still, I will think of you all the time. It is so sweet of you to remember me on my birthday. I was so busy that day I didn't know it was my birthday till 3 in the afternoon. The pipe is a beauty. Being your present, it will make many a peaceful, happy smoke for me whenever I smoke it.... The little yellow buds you put in your last letter made me think of our front porch, and of how beautiful it must be just now with its wealth of them.... I send you my picture taken the other day by an artist in Key West. I am afraid they are not good likenesses, for I am much thinner on account of the heat and look much older for whatever reason..... I am well, however, and stronger than I ever was, so you can know that I go to war in good condition....I am so glad you are well. Please don't be uneasy on my account; as I said before, the chance of war after all is a rather scant one......I must close now...... It is a pleasure to tell you that I am thinking about you all the time."

April 21st, '98: (Written from Key West, Fla.): "We are under orders to stand by to leave to-night.......I felt like I would like to write you a line before going, to say good-bye, not that there is any danger for me—there never is any—but I knew you would wish to hear. For your sake, I might almost wish there would be no war; on my own account, I am very happy that chance is offered me for distinction. ... You need have no fear for me. Nothing will happen to me with such prayers as yours to aid me. I shall have full confidence at all times, in action or wherever I may be, and that alone would keep me ready to do good service... Our boat is in splendid condition, and officers and men are well and anxious for a fight. We have good men and faithful ones, and our chances for success are the very best...... Do not be afraid for me. Everything turns out for the best."

May 4th, '98: (Written from Key West): "We leave in a few hours for Matanzas, whence we came two days ago for some minor repairs and necessary stores and coal. You are the sweetest mother to me, for more reasons than I can ever count; but I am thinking principally about your writing to me. Everytime we have received a mail there has been a letter from you; and you would be so glad if you knew how happy they make me. Each time we come into port or get any chance whatever to send you a letter I shall do so, and have done so up to this moment.

"You need have no fears about me, for there is no danger for us now. There may be when the Spanish fleet comes, but I am sorry to say that I fear that will never be. A war comes only once in a generation, and it will be very hard if I can get no chance to do some unusual service, so it is very disappointing to have no tangible enemy to meet. You are a brave mother, so you must feel like I do whenever we are engaged in anything at all dangerous—enjoy the excitement, feel that, but nothing more. Thank heaven, I have found that I have no fear, for I have analyzed all my feelings in danger. Don't repeat that, it would be a boast to anyone but you. Your last letter made me feel so happy and I am so proud to receive your praise, to feel that never have I 'given you an hour's trouble or unhappiness.' To hear you say that, dear angel, is more to me than any ambition in this world.

"Do you ever think that I have no heart to love because I follow a profession that keeps me nearly always from you? I know that you never do feel so, for you know I love you. Sometimes I remember and think of how you always love to have us children tell you how much we love you and how you used to wonder why I hardly ever petted you. When I am away it is so easy to write my thoughts to you as they come and tell you how I yearn to be with you. But when with you, it is my reverence for you that keeps me back, quiet but (even if I do say it) waiting to serve you, not as a return, but in appreciation of the tender loving care and the hard sacrifices that not till late (years too late) have I understood; I can indeed, my mother, 'rise up and call you blessed.'....Good bye for a short space. This letter is hurried for there is a great deal that I must do. Love to everyone........Good bye for a few days."

The following is his last letter, which was received by his mother half an hour after the news that prostrated her. It was dated "Off Matanzas, Cuba, May 7th, 1898, 11.30 a. m."

"We are now lying off Matanzas in the middle of the entrance to the harbor three miles further in. A mile and a half away on one side are the Panto Gardia and Sabanilla batteries, and at the same distance on the other side are the Maya and other batteries. Matanzas is a town of about 35,000 inhabitants with an antebellum commerce of some value. It lies, as I said before, three miles inside the entrance at which we are lying, around a horse shoe or bend which makes it not visible from our position. The batteries, however, are here at the entrance and made themselves very much in evidence yesterday by firing at the Dupont, which was lying too close under their fire. She got away quickly and in return for having to run, went up the coast two miles and leveled a Spanish block-house. The Winslow has not been fired at. All the large ships here left the blockade, the gunboats and torpedo boats remaining to hold it. No ship has as much as hove in sight of this entrance for days. So you may judge for yourself whether the blockade is effective.

"The work, I must say, is extremely tough and unpleasant. We are in great luck when we receive newspapers from the news correspondents three days after they are published, and read news greedily.

"Being without news and nothing happening within our own little sphere, the monotony is absolutely painful. There are two other warships here, the torpedo boat Dupont, and the armed yacht Hornet. These two boats lie over at the eastern entrance, while we guard the western. Of course it is necessary to keep a very careful lookout at night on account of the Spanish gunboats in these waters. The calibre of their guns is greater than that of our three little 1-pounders, but we wish they would come out just the same, for we would use our torpedoes and sink them ... You may be sure, I am well. The weather is not half bad, as we use the awnings now and get all the breeze without the sun. It is nearly always perfectly clear and a light passing shower this morning is the first rain I have seen since the beginning of the war.

"No one knows where the armored ships of our squadron have gone, but it is supposed that they have left to intercept the Spanish fleet off San Juan, should that port prove to be its destination.

"The nation as a whole, from the tenor of the papers, has realized that the navy is our defense, our real fighting body.." .....

"The Navy has shown its worth; we may trust hereafter that politicians will cease to prate as they did six months ago, about our 'expensive gold-laced luxury'. Our nation, a first.class power supposedly, should at the present moment feel shame that our navy is not such a one that the war should even now be over. To me it seems a disgrace that the United States should be fighting an apparently lengthy war with a nation poor in defense as well as finances. How can the ordinarily well-informed man, although he may have some pride of country, tingle with it as he should, if such conditions last? It is this 'rope-rein' politics, advanced by dishonest 'leg-pulling' demagogues, that keeps us as a nation from gaining and gaining glory 'till we forget'. I have almost spoken my thoughts on paper, and have forgotten that I am writing a letter. The above subject, which so absorbed me, is close to my heart......The Dupont is coming this way, so I must have my letter ready for her and close now. I feel that I will hear from you when the next mail comes. Bless you, dear, for your goodness.

"Love to each one, and don't forget that I am in perfect safety.

"Devotedly,

"WORTH."

## CHAPTER VI

### AT CARDENAS.

ON the 11th of May, the telegraphic reports conveyed the news that the Winslow had been engaged near Cardenas with three Spanish gun-boats. The Associated Press account, dated May 10th, was as follows:

"On board the Associated Press dispatch boat Kate Spencer, off Cardenas, May 9th, (via Key West, Fla.)—May 10th.—The little torpedo boat Winslow yesterday morning precipitated the first naval engagement fought in Cuban waters. On a reconnoissance in Cardenas Harbor she drew the fire of three Spanish coast guard vessels, and a lively vest pocket sea fight followed with the tiny gun boats. As the Winslow was decidedly in the minority she ran for the open sea, where her big station mate, the gun boat Machias, who had been called up by the firing, took a hand in the game with her four inch rifles and tossed several shells over the low sand spit behind which Spanish boats were sheltered. It was impossible to see whether any of these landed. The Winslow was not touched, but she claims to have knocked a few splinters out of the larger coast guard boat.

"The most important result of the Winslow's reconnoissance was the discovery that Cardenas harbor is mined. If there were any batteries on shore, the Spaniards did not think it worth while to disclose their position. That there are mines in the channel, is important in view of the report that it is Cardenas and not Matanzas, where the landing of United States forces will be made.

"The fight with the Guardia Costas occurred yesterday morning. Cardenas is one of the largest bays along the coast, the little town of the same name, lying at the southern end. From the western shore Icicas Point reaches out like a long index finger, almost touching Piedras Key Light, which in peaceful days beaconed the harbor entrance. The light house has been in darkness and deserted for many nights.

"Feeling safe in the desolation of the light house and the silence ashore, the little Winslow crept quietly in, under the early morning haze, for a closer inspection of the harbor. There had evidently been a lookout among the dunes along the sand spit, for the Winslow was allowed to feel her way into the harbor, taking notes of changed buoys and false marks designed to lead a hostile fleet on to torpedo fields. But, suddenly, there was a puff of smoke among the mangrove clumps along one of the inlets and a six pound shell screeched out of the bushes. Crack! came another from the shelter of a tiny key in the bay, and a third from further down the coast. Then three coast guard boats darted from their cover, under a full head of steam, like a big garpike after a minnow. The Winslow's crew jumped to the two pounders fore and aft and let the Spaniards have it, port and star-board, as they chased in. The little gun boats came along, shooting, but after the usual Spanish fashion, hit nothing but the adjacent scenery. Then the Winslow scuttled along for the open sea, using her after gun as a stern chaser and defiantly shooting as she went along. The Spanish boats wasted about sixty shots, and the biggest boat, mounting a twelve pounder, kept up the bombardment as long as the Winslow was in range. The Spaniards who had probably heard the news from Manila, were evidently as mad as a nest of hornets and kept up the chase until all four of the little craft were rocking in the swell past Piedras Keys. Just then there was a crash and a roar to seaward and the Machias, bearing in under a canopy of smoke, sent a shell smashing into the pursuing fleet. The little patrol boats spun about like water spiders and ran to shelter beyond the sand spit. The Machias sent a few shells skipping in between the sand dunes, but with what effect could not be seen.

"At any rate, there are three prospective additions to our mosquito fleet bottled up in Cardenas harbor, waiting shipment."

This news deepened the anxiety in the home of Ensign Bagley, though the retreat of the Winslow in good order was regarded as a sign that it could take care of itself. Prayers of thanksgiving went up for the successful termination of this first engagement in Cuban waters. There was no thought that the engagement was to be repeated, and when the news of the result of the battle on May 11th, was flashed to Raleigh, the blow was as crushing as if no news of the first fight had been received. Thursday, May 12th, on the sweetest of May mornings, as Mrs. Bagley and family were at a late breakfast, talking of the happy escape from the fight of May 8th, the door-bell rang. Hon. W. M. Russ, Mayor of the city, had called at Mrs. Bagley's home to break the terrible news contained in this telegram ;

        KEY WEST, FLA., May 12th, 1898.
MAYOR OF RALEIGH :—
 Please break news to Mrs. Bagley that her son was killed instantly in action off Cardenas yesterday.
          JOHN B. BERNADOU.

 The Mayor, long a friend of the family and of the young officer, with a heavy heart, first communicated the news to this writer. It was feared that the mother, not fully recovered from her serious illness of 1897, could not survive the shock, and it was not until her physician, Dr. Hubert Haywood, had been hastily summoned, that it was deemed safe to acquaint her with the contents of the telegram. The universal sympathy, so prompt and touching, coming first from all the people of Raleigh, and later from all portions of the country, carried a measure of consolation and comfort that helped to temper the blow.

 From a letter written by Lieutenant Bernadou, commander of the Winslow, to Mr. W. H. Bagley, brother of Ensign Worth Bagley, the following extracts, telling of the engagement, are taken :

 "I have deemed it best to wait, before writing you, until I have sufficiently convalesced to be myself again. Your brother had become a proven friend, and the remembrance of his loss awakens a keener pang than the sense of my bodily injury. Still, life is short for all of us ; he fell in harness ; and the Almighty has bestowed upon him the great honor of calling upon him to die for his country,—than which no honor is greater.

 "Your brother died instantly. I was standing about ten feet from him when he fell and immediately ran to him. A glance conveyed the impression that life was extinct, and a minute's observation confirmed the impression. A hasty examination of his wounds showed me that there was nothing to be done to save him. His face was composed ; I do not believe that he suffered. The remains were immediately removed to the most protected spot and covered. Directly after the fight I signaled to the Wilmington: 'Send boat with doctor, many killed and wounded'; and upon transferring those that were injured, I took your brother's body with me and saw it placed upon the quarter deck and covered with the flag, before having my own wound dressed.

 "Your brother fell at the end of the action. Injuries to the machinery and steering gear had made the boat almost unmanageable. As I found that we were working out from under the enemy's batteries by alternately backing and going ahead with the one remaining engine, and as mechanical communication with the engine room was cut off, I directed him to watch the movement of the vessel ; to keep her out of the Wilmington's line of fire ; to watch the man at the reversing gun below and see that he obeyed orders. This necessitated your brother making repeated short trips from the deck to the foot of the engine room ladder. On the conclusion of one of these trips, he had stopped for a moment on deck, presumably to watch the effect of our (the Wilmington's) fire, which was silencing the enemy. He came up to me where I was standing, near the compass forward, and said: 'Captain, I'm sorry you're wounded; I'm lucky in these things.' I replied: 'Well, old man, we've been in a fight this time for sure.' He said: 'Shake'; and we shook hands and looked one another full in the eyes. A moment later was a quick explosion,—a short snap, like the report of a pistol; your brother and two fell dead; and two were mortally wounded.

"After being conveyed to the Wilmington, your brother's body was transferred to the revenue cutter Hudson and arrived at Key West on the morning of the 12th. Being anxious to convey to your mother the news of the death of her son, and to minimize the chance of its coming to her indirectly; and not having your address at hand, I wired to the Mayor of Raleigh. At about the same time I learned that Paymaster Izard had notified General Breckinridge, requesting him to break the news to her. I trust that what I did was for the best.

"The funeral of your brother here took place on the 13th, when the rites were celebrated in accordance with the service of the Episcopal church......Here at Key West, every officer's wife present, every officer and all the men of the torpedo fleet, vied with one another in bestowing affectionate care and attention to all that remained to us of one so generally beloved, respected and admired. And apart from personal feelings, I cannot but deplore the loss to the service of such a gallant fellow, the embodiment of all that a young officer should be, and who served as a model for the best half of the juniors of the fleet.

"I have been in intimate contact with your brother for nearly five months; have practically had no other companion; was dependent upon him for many things, and it is not so easy for me to write to you ..... The general accounts of the fight published were garbled....Your brother did not fall overboard, as stated, nor was he killed in attempting to reach any tow line; he died instantly at his post, while observing the movements of the enemy. To the moment of his end he was as cool and collected as when demonstrating his splendid abilities and judgment on the field of athletic contest."

Lieutenant Bernadou's official report of the engagement to the Secretary of the Navy in full, is as follows:

CONVENT HOSPITAL, Key West, Fla., May 16th, 1898.
THE HONORABLE SECRETARY OF THE NAVY:
SIR—

1. I respectfully submit the following report of the action off Cardenas, Cuba, as participated in by the U. S. torpedo boat Winslow, to supplement the summarized statement submitted by me on the 11th inst., the day of the fight.

2. The Winslow arrived off Cardenas from Matanzas at 9 a. m. on the 11th, having left her station on the blockade to obtain an additional supply of coal, the amount of fuel in her bunkers being reduced to five tons. The U. S. S. Machias and Wilmington were found at Peidras Cay. Upon making application to Captain Merry the senior officer present, I was directed to apply to Captain Todd, commanding U. S. S. Wilmington, for necessary supplies.

3. On boarding the U. S. S. Wilmington, I was informed by her commanding officer of his intention to enter Cardenas harbor on the afternoon of that day. Of the three channels leading through the Cays, two were believed to be mined; there remained unexplored a third channel between Romero and Blanco Cays, over which the minimum depth of water, as shown by the chart, was one and three-quarter fathoms. As the rise of tide at this place was about one and one-half feet, and as the Wilmington drew scant ten feet, I was directed to receive on board a Cuban pilot, Santos, to take with me the revenue cutter Hudson to sweep the channel for torpedoes. This work I completed by noon, except the sweeping of the channel, which could not be done on account of the grounding of the Hudson. That vessel touched lightly but managed to work off without injury. The Winslow, therefore, dragged the channel with grapnels and returned to the Wilmington, reporting to Captain Todd upon the practicability of the entrance.

4. The entrance was begun at 12:30, high tide, the Hudson on the starboard side and the Winslow on the port side of the Wilmington assisting in marking out shoal water. No vessels were in sight on entering Cardenas bay, save two square-rigged merchantmen with sails unbent, anchored directly off the town. As it was thought possible that gunboats might attempt to escape, the Hudson was sent along the western side and the eastern side of the bay to intercept them in event of such movement; not finding them, the three vessels met off the town at a distance of about 3500 yards. When in this position, the Winslow was signalled to approach the Wilmington within hail and I was directed by Captain Todd to go in and investigate a small gunboat then observed for the first time,—painted grey, with black smokestack, apparently not under steam and moored to a wharf, to the left of which arose a compact mass of buildings close to the water front. Torpedoes were set for surface runs, the fans upon the war noses were run up, so as to provide for explosion at short range for use alongside of the gunboat, and all preparations were made for immediate action.

5. At a distance of about 1500 yards, at which time the Winslow was advancing about 12 knots, which seems her maximum speed in quite shoal water, the first gun of the engagement was fired from the bow of the Spanish gunboat, marked by a clear puff of white smoke. This shot, which passed over the Winslow, was at once replied to by that ship and was the signal for the commencement from the beach of a rapidly sustained fire, characterized primarily by a total absence of smoke. At the commencement of this firing, I received a flesh wound in the left thigh. As the action advanced, a cloud of haze collected on shore at the location of this battery, and when closest I detected one or two gun flashes from among the buildings, but at no time could I detect the exact position of the guns. My uncertainty as to the position of the enemy was attested to by the commanding officer of the Hudson and by officers commanding gun divisions on the Wilmington, who enquired of me shortly after the action what I made out to be the enemy's exact position.

6. At this time the wind was blowing from the ships toward the shore. The first shot that pierced the Winslow rendered her steam and hand steering gear inoperative and damaged them beyond repair. Efforts to work the hand steering gear from aft were frustrated by the wrecking of that mechanism and the rupture of both wheel ropes; relieving tackles failed to operate the rudder. For a short time the vessel was held in her bows on position by use of her propellers. She then swung broadside to the enemy. A shot now pierced her engine room, rendering one engine inoperative. I directed my attention to maintaining fire from her

1-pounder guns, to keeping the vessel constantly in movement, so as to reduce the chances of her being hit, to endeavoring to withdraw from close range and to keeping clear of the line of fire of the Wilmington and Hudson. The use of the remaining engine, however, had the effect of throwing her stern towards the enemy upon backing, while going ahead threw her bow in the same direction. Under the heavy fire of the Wilmington the fire of the enemy slackened; the Spanish gunboat was silenced and put out of action early in the engagement.

7. The Winslow now being practically disabled, I signalled to the Hudson to tow us out of action; she very gallantly approached us and we succeeded in getting a line to her. Previous to this, the alternate rapid backing and steaming ahead of the Winslow had had the effect of working her out from under the enemy's batteries, and in this way a distance of about 300 yards was gained. Finding that we were working out in this manner, I directed Ensign Bagley to concentrate his attention upon the movement of the ship, watching the vessel so as to keep her out of the Wilmington's way and to direct the movements of the man at the reversing gear, mechanical communication from deck to engine being impracticable. This necessitated Mr. Bagley's making repeated short trips from the deck to the foot of the engine room ladder. While directing the vessel's course and at the moment of being on deck, he stood abreast of the starboard gun, close to a group of men who had been stationed below, but who had been sent on deck from the disabled machinery. A shell hitting, I believe, a hose-reel, exploded instantly, killing Ensign Bagley and two others and mortally wounding two. This accident, which occurred at the close of the action, was virtually its end; the enemy fired a few more shots, but was soon completely silenced by the heavy firing of the Wilmington. The conduct of Ensign Bagley and of the men with him as well as that of the crew who survived the fight, is beyond commendation. After seeing the dead and wounded removed from the Winslow and conveyed on board the Wilmington, I turned over the command of the ship to Gunner's Mate G. P. Brady, my own injury preventing me from performing active duty for the time being.

I have the honor to remain, sir,
Your obedient servant,
JOHN B. BERNADOU,
Lieut., U. S. Navy.

The papers published many and varied accounts of the engagement. The official report here given makes it necessary to print but one newspaper extract. Concluding a graphic account in the New York Journal, dated Key West, May 12th, Mr. Vincent S Cooke writes:

"The engagement at Cardenas was not a lost fight by any means although the ships withdrew in caring for the Winslow. The Spanish loss in killed and wounded is not known, but the chances are that it will be soon. It is said that the Machias and Wilmington were to enter the harbor and shell Cardenas at once.

"The death of these men has cast a gloom over the people here. All Flags are at half-mast. Ensign Bagley is well known, and while the fleet was here was a general favorite. He was known as a fearless young officer and was well thought of by his superiors. Captain Todd, of the Wilmington, who gave the order to go into Cardenas Harbor, was especially fond of Bagley, and more than once, in speaking of the young officer, said: "He's got the right material in him."

"Lieutenant Bernadou was also fond of Bagley. The men on the Hudson say they never saw greater courage than Bagley and his men exhibited while standing unprotected on the Winslow, waiting to catch the Hudson's line. The air was full of shots, and every instant was fraught with danger, but Bagley coolly stood by his men, knowing that unless a line was gotten the Winslow would be shot into ribbons and sunk.

"Describing the fight, Captain Newcomb of the Hudson said:

"We were in a trap. There were masked batteries at several points, and neither the Machias nor the Wilmington could aid us much, owing to the shallow water. Batteries opened on us from all sides—behind trees, bushes, houses and other places. I think the guns used by the masked batteries were field pieces."

Cardenas is an important point. It is pronounced Kar-day-nas, accent on the first syllable. It means "of a purple color." Cardenas Bay, in which the encounter took place, is a picturesque harbor, 70 miles west of Havana. It is broad and shallow, with two jutting fangs of land close at the mouth and a picket line of coral keys outside, and its surface is studded with other green crowned keys, through which the tortuous channel, scarce two fathoms deep, winds and twists its way to where the city of Cardenas lies nestled under the angle of the sloping hills, fully seven miles from the entrance. Its value to the American cause and General Lee's estimate of Ensign Bagley, are thus given in the Washington (D. C.) Times of May 13th:

"Maj. Gen. Fitzhugh Lee, who is spoken of as the most likely man for the post of military governor of Cuba until the republic is established firmly, said yesterday that Cardenas, which was attacked yesterday by four American gunboats, was an important point, strategetically, to be possessed by the United States forces.

"About twenty miles back in the country, at Jovellenes, I think it is, all the railroads of Cuba form a juncture, and, with Cardenas in the hands of the Americans, the investment of Havana would be materially advanced by the possession of that place," said Gen. Lee. "No supplies could reach Havana by the regular channels from the interior, and, with the blockading fleet in front of the city, its fate would soon be determined finally. In my opinion, the attack upon Cardenas was for the purpose of getting at Jovellenes.

"Gen. Lee was told that the official dispatches gave the number of killed as five and of wounded as three. Referring to Ensign Bagley, Gen. Lee said:

"He was a gallant lad, and I am sorry he is gone. He was a worthy fellow and brave as a lion. I'll bet he made a good fight. But we must not take our losses too much to heart. War means blood-shed upon both sides, and we are bound to lose many brave lads before we drag down the yellow ensign of Spain from the ramparts of Morro."

In Collier's Weekly of June 4th, Mr. James H. Hare, staff photographer, writing of an expedition to Gomez's camp, tells of an adventure with the Winslow, as his party was trying to escape the Spaniards to reach an American ship :

"Suddenly we saw smoke in the distance ; it was evident we had been sighted. The outlines of a boat appeared. Then smoke became more distinct. The boat was certainly bearing down on us. What was it. Our glasses were trained on it. It loomed up, larger and larger. "bow on" all the time, so we could not decide whether it was a Spanish gunboat or one of our own craft, until at last "Old Glory" was recognized and our anxiety was at an end.

"Bang!" went a shot. We hove to immediately. "Bang!" went another, evidently a shotted gun, by the sound.

"Let down your sails!" we shouted to the sailor. "Hurry up!" That is an American expression, but he understood it.

"By this time we personally had been recognized, and as we lay to, awaiting instructions from the torpedo boat, we sang the Doxology— perhaps not very musically, but I will guarantee with as much sincerity as it had ever known, for our own "Winslow" now had us in charge.

"We were taken to the "Machias," where the captain and officers made us very welcome, and food was set before us that we shall never forget, for it was the first civilized meal we had eaten in two weeks.

"We joked the "Winslow's" officers, Lieutenant Bernadou and Ensign Bagley, about the prize they thought they had in view when they bore down on us. This was on Sunday, May 8. On the following Thursday I photographed the remains of Ensign Bagley and some of his crew and later attended their funeral : they had been killed in action off Cardenas—"the fortunes of war," with a vengeance."

The New York Herald's staff correspondent, sent an interview that was published May 13th, with Ensign Bagley, indicating that he had premonitions of the fate that was in store for him :

"KEY WEST, FLA., Thursday.—The death of Ensign Bagley recalls a story written after an interview with him on April 29, which was suppressed by the censor, who feared that it might cause Bagley's friends unnecessary alarm.

"From the HERALD's despatch boat Albert F. Dewey I had boarded the Winslow to take papers and news bulletins to Lieutenant Bernadon. After talking some minutes with him I turned to Ensign Bagley with some remark about the troubles which had befallen his fellow executive officers of the torpedo fleet. His rejoinder was :—

"Yes, I hear that Boyd (of the torpedo boat Cushing) is in trouble through no fault of his own. That puts it right up to me. I'm sorry about Boyd, for I am sure that the accident to the Cushing was not due to his carelessness. Now, I suppose you will say that I am superstitious but I must admit that the fatalities which have pursued us have given me some moments of sombre thought.

"'There was poor Breckinridge, my classmate, executive officer of the Cushing, who was swept overboard between Key West and Havana and drowned. Then Bostwick, executive officer of the Ericsson, who was knocked overboard in a collision with a schooner, had his chest caved in and was all but drowned. He is now slowly recovering. Baldwin, executive officer of the Cushing, successor of Breckinridge and predecessor of Boyd, took his turn next. He was knocked down an open hatchway and had his ribs broken. He will not be out of the hospital until the war is over.

"There they are, the four 'B's'—Breckinridge, Bostwick, Baldwin and Boyd. I am the fifth and last—Bagley. I have never been superstitious, but for a week I have had mysterious intuitions that I am not to escape. I will make the list complete—of that I am certain. I only hope that my trouble will not be serious enough to take me out of the fight."

"Bagley's closing remarks were made in a laughing manner, as though he would not have me take them seriously. Yet it was easily seen that the premonition of serious trouble had taken a strong hold upon him. At any rate, the fate of the 'B's' is complete, and the torpedo boats are now expected by the "jackies," who are always superstitious, to have better luck in the future."

## CHAPTER VII.

### ANTE-BURIAL SERVICE AT KEY WEST.

THE body of the young Ensign was carried to Key West, where it was embalmed. There, as well as all other points where his ship had headquarters, he had made warm friends. The officer ordered by the Navy Department to accompany the body from Key West to Raleigh was at Cardenas and did not receive the orders in time. The exigencies of the war thus preventing a naval funeral at his home, the authorities at Key West arranged to have ante-burial services in that place on the afternoon of May 13th. These services were held by Rev. Gilbert Higgs, rector of St. Paul's Protestant Episcopal church, who had formerly been rector at Jackson and Warrenton, N. C. From a letter, dated May 14th written by Dr. Higgs to Rev. Dr. M. M. Marshall, rector of Christ church, Raleigh, these extracts are taken:

"Yesterday I read the ante burial service over the remains of the late Ensign Worth Bagley, Raleigh, N. C. He was the first officer killed in battle in our war with Spain .... I write to you thinking it might be a comfort to his parents and family to hear through you that his remains were sent to them from God's house and to know that not only a large representation of the Navy and Army, but many of our citizens were present in the church and afterwards in a procession, the casket covered with flowers and emblems, the body was borne to the steamer leaving that evening for Tampa..... For many things I love North Carolina, its people, and feel it an honor to the State that she can claim the first martyr in the nation's call to arms, and it is a great satisfaction to me to have been here to minister the last rites before the interment."

The following is the Associated Press telegram giving an account of the funeral at Key West:

"KEY WEST, Fla., May 15th.

"The remains of Ensign Worth Bagley, of the torpedo boat Winslow, were sent to Jacksonville this evening to his brother there, from which point they will be taken to his home in Raleigh, N. C. Brief funeral services were held at St. Paul's Episcopal church, the Rev. Dr. Gilbert Higgs officiating. A number of officers, with a guard of marines and sailors from many ships, escorted the body to the church. The Stars and Stripes and a number of floral offerings covered the coffin. At the conclusion of the services many passed near the casket to take a last look upon the face of the dead. The casket was borne by six sailors, immediately followed by the pall bearers selected from among Ensign Bagley's personal friends. Then came fifteen survivors of the torpedo boat Winslow, who showed much emotion as they gazed upon the dead officer.

"Most of the fleet officers attended the services and marched to the wharf. A salute was given when the body was placed on the steamer Mascotte."

The New York World's account of the funeral contains these additional particulars:

"The commander and executive officer of every warship in Key West harbor was in the procession, and all lifted their gold-embroidered caps and stood in attention as the body passed.

"Worth Bagley was the first officer of the United States to fall in a naval engagement of the present war.

"Only a few weeks ago he remarked: 'It is the ambition of my life to have a shot at Spain.'

"He had that one shot, and it cost him his life.

"While at Annapolis he played on the foot-ball eleven. For two years he was full-back, and men who were plebes when he was an upper classman will tell you to-day that no one ever went to Annapolis who could play foot-ball like Bagley. He graduated in 1895 and was on the Maine, until Commander Bernadou, of the Winslow, sent for him and made him executive officer, a great honor for an Ensign of twenty-four.

"At Annapolis the three greatest cronies were Breckinridge, Merritt and Bagley. Breckinridge was washed overboard and drowned from the deck of the torpedo boat Cushing in a storm just outside of Morro Castle, Merritt went down with the Maine and his body was never recovered."

In the account in the Washington Times, still more particulars are given:

"The body was escorted to the church and thence to the boat by a guard of fifty marines, and an equal number of blue jackets from the torpedo boats now in the harbor, including a color-guard for the draped flag.

"Ten junior officers acted as honorary pall bearers. The coffin was covered with the flag, on which the dead man's sword rested among flowers."

Among the tender letters received by his mother was one from a Key West lady, at whose home he had spent the last evening ashore. Under date of May 14th, she writes:

"The precious remains of your son were taken to our church, St. Paul's, yesterday afternoon. The casket was borne by eight sailors from his ship; it was draped with his flag, and kind hearts placed on it God's choicest gifts, sweet flowers. The church was filled with sympathizing friends who, after the service, followed the body to the steamer.... The beautiful hymn sung at the service was: 'When our heads are bowed with woe.'"

Capt. C. M. Chester, commander of the U. S. S. Cincinnati, writing from Key West, Fla., on May 13th, to Mrs. Bagley, gives an account of the funeral and his estimate of the young Ensign:

"It was my sad yet agreeable duty to have charge of the ceremonies attending the funeral of your son Worth to-day, and they were made more sad and also more agreeable by the fact that he was under my care as Commandant of Cadets at Annapolis for nearly four years. There I learned to have a high regard for his manly and sterling qualities, and I always felt that whatever difficulties came up his honor and integrity could be relied upon.

"Full of courage and youthful vigor, he has met the death that we who are approaching the three score years limit of life, envy. Yet, for him with his life all before him, we almost doubt the Divine will that orders such things. We must, however, bow to it, and I trust the Father who doeth all things well will give you strength to bear this great affliction. May He comfort you with the thought that you have such a noble boy, and with the knowledge that all his friends loved him...... With great respect for the mother of one so worthy."

Writing under date of May 16th, at Key West, Fla., Mr. Walter B. Izard, of the U. S. S. Machias, who had been a class-mate of Ensign Bagley's at Annapolis, says:

"I was ordered by the Department to accompany his body North, but as we have only just returned from Cardenas, I did not receive them. I would like to have done something for him at the last......Everything that was possible was done......I want to express my deepest sympathy for you at the loss of your noble son. I had known Worth so long and intimately that it seems hard to realize that so true an officer should be taken from us."

The casket containing all that was mortal of Ensign Worth Bagley, U. S. N., reached Jacksonville Sunday morning. To that point the oldest brother of the dead officer had come to take home the body of the noble youth who had given up his life for his country.

## CHAPTER VIII.

### THE FUNERAL IN RALEIGH.

THE following account, with a few additions, of the funeral held in Capitol Square, Raleigh, N. C., at the foot of Houdon's statue of Washington, Monday afternoon May 16th, is taken from Tuesday morning's News and Observer:

"Yesterday afternoon at 5 o'clock when the funeral open air exercises were in progress in the capitol square, over the body of Ensign Bagley, the United States flag over the quaint old building was exultant in the sweet wind from the south.

"It seemed typical of the pride of this great nation in the thrilling valor of this youth from the Old North State.

"There he lay under the tall green elms the casket wrapped in colors overlaid with spear of palm and wreath of ivy. The casket rested on a caisson-shaped pedestal.

"It contained the body of Worth Bagley, Ensign, U. S. N., Torpedo Boat Winslow, killed May 11th, in an action off Cardenas, while at his post of duty,

"At 1.30 p. m. a detail of forty-eight men from the Governor's Guard, Co. K, as a special escort, accompanied the remains to the capitol from the home of Mrs Bagley. The casket wrapped in a large United States flag, completely covered with beautiful floral decorations, was lifted on the shoulders of six non-commissioned officers, chosen to act as body bearers, Sergeants Bunch, Broughton, Remington, Snipe, Perry and Hughes, and borne from the home and placed on the caisson, which was draped in black. Its six horses had also black coverings and each was led by a United States soldier. They were followed by the following officers of the First and Second Regiments of North Carolina Volunteers, who acted as honorary pall-bearers: Capt. Crawford, of the Governor's Guard, Raleigh ; Capt. Robertson, of the Hornets' Nest Rifles, Charlotte ; Capt. Michie, of the Durham Light Infantry ; Capt. MacRae, of the Wilmington Light Infantry ; Capt. Bain, of the Goldsboro Rifles ; Capt. Gray, of the Guilford Grays, Greensboro. The caisson, completely covered with flowers, accompanied by the military escort, moved slowly to the capitol. Along Fayetteville street the cortege moved with grim bareness, the honors being those of a Brigadier General. As the caisson passed along heads were bowed and bared before the loved boy to whom those of his home were glad to do such honor, and the sidewalks were deep with the people and the windows sombre with the tears on the faces of women.

"The body at the capitol, in the rotunda under the dome, for two hours lay in state, though the face was not exposed, and while this was justly considered wise, it may be grateful to friends to say that the face was splendid to look upon and not disfigured. as has been incorrectly sent out by the press. Floral designs were sent up from the home by the wagon load, and were eagerly taken by loving hands, men, women and children alike, and disposed about the circular area under the dome. Elaborate designs had been sent by friends, cities and organizations from

SNAP SHOTS—FOOT-BALL FIELD AND SUMMER CRUISE.
SPOILING A SNAP BACK. (BAGLEY AT RIGHT END OF CROWD.)
NAVY GOES AROUND THE END FOR TEN YARDS. (BAGLEY AT CENTRE, TO LEFT OF REFEREE.)
SUMMER CRUISE ON "CONSTELLATION." (BAGLEY AND BRECKINRIDGE IN WORKING SUITS.)
BAGLEY AND IZARD IN POSITION FOR PLACE KICK FOR GOAL. (BAGLEY STANDING.)

all parts of the country. Remaining under charge of the military detail, the casket was viewed by thousands of people who walked reverently through the corridors of the capitol until the arrival of the Brigade at 3.30 p. m.

"All places of business in the city were closed promptly at 4 o'clock and shortly after that hour the reverent throng withdrew from the rotunda and corridors that the family might be alone with their dead.

"Soon the casket was again lifted on the shoulders of the soldier-body-bearers. Preceded by all of the city clergy and several ministers from a distance, all reading in unison the solemn and beautiful scripture, beginning 'I am the Resurrection and the Life,' and followed by the family, the body was borne along the line of the special escort, which was standing with 'present arms' formation to the catafalque at the south end of the broad terrace which overlooked the length of Fayetteville street. The family, with its large connection was seated on the right of the casket, the ministers in the rear, immediately in front of the statue of Washington. On the left were the choir, the honorary pall-bearers, and behind them the State and City officials, State Supreme Court and Federal judges, and the class-mates of Ensign Bagley at Morson and Denson's Academy. Around were delegations from many towns and cities, students from Morson's Academy, children of the Centennial and Murphey graded schools, and young ladies of Peace Institute and St. Mary's. Outside of all those who had been assigned places nearest the remains, the battalion of cadets from the Agricultural and Mechanical college, under command of Major Stancell, were formed in a large circle. Beyond these were the students of Shaw University, and the children of Garfield and Washington graded schools, and the thousands of men, women and children from a hundred towns, cities and hamlets who had gathered to join with the people of Raleigh to pay honor to Raleigh's noble martyr-hero.

"The Brigade, including the First and Second Regiments of North Carolina Volunteers, under command of Colonel Armfield, was formed on Fayetteville street.

"The funeral services were conducted by Rev. Eugene Daniel, D. D., pastor of the First Presbyterian church, of which Ensign Bagley was a member, assisted by Rev. W. C. Norman, D D., pastor of Edenton Street Methodist church; Rev. M. M. Marshall, D. D., rector of Christ Protestant Episcopal church, and Rev. Thos. E. Skinner, D. D., of the Baptist church. The choir consisted of the following persons: Mrs. M. P. Baumann, Mrs. J. J Thomas, Mrs. D. H. Hamilton, Mrs. Chas. McKimmon, Miss Minnie Tucker, Miss Potter. Miss Bessie Bates. Miss Ada Womble, Miss Josephine Mitchell, Miss Mary Dinwiddie, Mr. W. S. Primrose, Mr. T. K. Bruner, Mr. Chas Newcomb, Mr. Leo D. Heartt, with accompanists. Miss Bettie Dinwiddie, organ, Mr. Sam Parrish, organ, and Mr. J. D. Turner, trombone.

"The services began with a hymn: "The Son of God Goes Forth to War," sung by the full choir, with organ and trombone accompaniment.

"Rev. Thos. E. Skinner, D. D., of the Baptist church, then offered an appropriate prayer.

"Mrs. Chas. McKimmon sang with touching pathos a favorite selection of Ensign Bagley, the music of which is by the wife of Commander Crowninshield, U. S. N.:

> "There is a land mine eye hath seen
> In visions of enraptured thought,
> So bright that all that spreads between
> Is with its radiant glory fraught.

A land upon whose blissful shore
There rests no shadow, falls no stain,
There those who meet shall part no more
And those long parted meet again

Its skies are not like earthly skies,
With varying hues of shade and light;
It hath no need of suns to rise
To dissipate the gloom of night.

There sweeps no desolating wind
Across the calm, serene abode;
A wanderer there a home may find
Within the paradise of God."

"Rev. W. C. Norman, D. D., of Edenton Street M. E. church, South, read the 90th Psalm, commencing 'Lord thou hast been our dwelling place in all generations.'

"A quartette, Mrs. Chas McKimmon, soprano; Mrs. J. J. Thomas, contralto; Mr. Chas. Newcomb, tenor, and Mr. W. S. Primrose, bass, then chanted the beautiful hymn:

"'Abide with Me, Fast Falls the Eventide.'

"Rev. Eugene Daniel, D. D., of the First Presbyterian church, read from the 15th chapter of 1st Corinthians, and offered a prayer so beautiful and appropriate that it is elsewhere in to-day's paper published in full. The choir then sang: 'Just As I Am, Without One Plea,' many soldiers (at the request of Ensign Bagley's mother, announced by Dr. Daniel) joining in the hymn.

"This strange summer scene of peace, with the great grove shot to the heart with requiems presented a startling contrast with the martial dead lying solitary in the midst of the great mass. But the contrast was no more marked than the blue of the sky with the black battalions of cloud that walked abroad war-voiced when the remains at midnight were nearing the city.

"The sky was rent with electric mines, and javelins of light alternated with terrible luminousness while silence was swallowed up in the deep-lunged fury of thunder.

"That was the music the young Ensign loved to hear, but no more than the sweet whispers of the elms of the capitol under which he had passed his childhood. For if he loved to revel breast high in danger, his life and letters showed that none was more soothed by the touch of gentleness and peace. Looking upon his face iron-lined with the curves of courage, some one remarked: 'There lies Napoleon.' Love took up the observation, saying: 'No, Napoleon had upon his face the look of an unsatisfied ambition; upon his face sleeps a smile of peace.' It was true, but illustrated just the contrast noted above wherein Love and War live together housed as one in the same heart.

"Ten thousand? Yes, more, said some. They stood surrounding the little funeral scene, lines of military diverging backward from the pulpit terrace. In front, down Fayetteville street, came the First and Second Regiments with a heavy tread.

"The services were over and the procession to Oakwood cemetery was forming. The band of the First Regiment was playing the 'Dead March in Saul', while eleven salutes were fired from a cannon at the east gate of the Capitol as the procession formed on Morgan street at the head of Fayetteville street, moving thence to Wilmington street, thence North street via North street to Oakwood avenue to Oakwood cemetery.

"'The dead march! Oh, the tears of the dead march! How it goes mourning through the grove trees of sweet Southern towns so poignantly when the dead is great in death.

"Along the route to the cemetery, the great line ebbed and flowed in motion, and thousands had taken their places along the way and on the hills overlooking beautiful Oakwood. All the city was mourning, the places of business had been closed, and there was no desire except to gather about the center of the common heart.

"Down the little hill, all knew so well, over the little rock bridge, the bridge of sighs to many a home, around the bend along the gentle slope, a gentle climb, there was the spot, the spot where his gallant father, Maj. W. H. Bagley, of the Confederate Army, lies, and where rest the dust of his honored and distinguished grandfather, Governor Jonathan Worth.

"As the family, the clergy and the pall-bearers surrounded the open grave, the picturesque hills that sloped off Oakwood being filled with a vast concourse of soldiers and citizens, the last sad rites were said. The impressive and touching prayer of committal was offered by Rev. M. M. Marshall, D. D., rector of Christ church, after which Rev. Eugene Daniel, D. D., pronounced the benediction.

"As they waited by the flower-lined grave, the choir sang softly without accompainment, 'Now the Day is Over', and one verse again of 'Abide with Me,' after which Mrs. J. J. Thomas, in the same key, sang sweetly the last sentence of a favorite song of Ensign Bagley 'Anchored', by Watson, as follows:

> "'A soft smile came from the stars,
> And a voice from the whisp'ring foam,
> Safe, safe at last, the danger past,
> Safe in his Father's home.'

The full choir responding ' Amen'.

"Once again and the last time the choir sang. This time the hymn called the ' Prayer for Seamen' of which the first verse is always used at the close of the chapel service at the Naval Academy where Ensign Bagley was a member of the choir:

> "'Eternal Father, strong to save,
> Whose arm hath bound the restless wave,
> Who bidd'st the mighty ocean deep
> Its own appointed limits keep;
> Oh, hear us when we cry to Thee
> For those in peril on the sea, Amen.'

"The flowers were nearby, ready to be disposed upon the grave, and they rose above the dead a very mass of tribute in color and sweetness, until the mound was hidden deep from the eye.

"From the capitol eleven guns had been fired, and now eleven more guns were fired at the cemetery.

"As the press of people fell away somewhat at the last words of the benediction, the troops were drawn up on the north side of the grave.

"The three volleys given over the body and commanded by Col. Armfield were stimulating to the hearts of those who heard in them an echo of the spirit of the dead.

"Taps were blown on the bugle from the head of the grave. There was a martial sweetness in the notes

"Worth Bagley, Ensign U. S. N., on Board Torpedo Boat Winslow, killed May 11th by a bursting shell in an action off Cardenas, while at post of duty.

"There he lay.

"The requiem of the elms had grown deeper with the deepening twilight.

"From the hearts of the thousands issued this inaudible chant: 'He lived well, he died well, he sleeps well!'

"The living had stood helpless in the presence of the dead that they would have brought back to life, but they stood mighty to do honor and that they had done for all the world to know."

## CHAPTER IX.

### HONORED IN RALEIGH.

RALEIGH was all tears, "like Niobe" when the announcement of the fatal engagement reached the city on Thursday morning, May 12th. The Post of the next morning told how the news was received in his native city:

"'Worth Bagley killed in a naval engagement in Cuban waters' were the words passed from mouth to mouth in Raleigh yesterday morning.

"'Never were the people of the capital city so shocked and never were there more spontaneous and genuine expressions of sympathy and grief expressed by all classes of people. As if by an electric current the news spread throughout the city and every heart throbbed in deepest sympathy for poor Worth Bagley and his grief-stricken mother, sisters and brothers. Everyone sought to discredit the news, hoping against hope that it was only a false report, but the bulletin boards soon announced confirmatory messages of the terrible tragedy in Cardenas harbor. Business was laid aside and people talked only of the distressing fate of the brave young naval officer. Since his enlistment in the navy the people of Raleigh, and of the State for that matter, have watched with pride and interest his position as a naval officer. They knew him as a boy, noble and brave in all things, and they knew furthermore that he was a worthy son of courageous and distinguished parentage. They knew the man, and they awaited only the opportunity for him to distinguish himself. Fate decreed otherwise. It remained for this brave young North Carolinian to be the first to sacrifice his life in the war against the Saffron flag. His death was that of a hero. It reads like a romance. It can hardly be realized."

A Saturday morning's issue of the News & Observer, in local columns, contained the following:

"There were yesterday inquires on every lip as to the details of the funeral ceremonies, and eulogy and distress throbbed even to the deep heart of the city. The sense of the heroic in men and women had glowed under the picture of the young officer's bearing in battle, but tears came when North Carolina took knowledge of the youth and promise of the son who had been torn asunder from her all too soon. Then, too, the home that had sent forth a mere youth who should in one brief hour thrill a nation's heart was turned to with tender condolence by scores of loving friends. All day long these friends called to offer their sympathy to those who mourned.

"Among those who came was a committee composed of Mayor Russ, Messrs. N. W. West, W. S. Primrose, R. T. Gray and F. A. Olds.

"These gentlemen brought the request that the family accede to the general desire for a military funeral. Furthermore, it was stated by the committee, that as no church in the city would begin to accommodate those who wished to attend the funeral, that the plan had been suggested to have the ceremonies in the Capitol grounds.

"Deeply touched by those expressions on the part of their own people, the family assented to the request."

The two thousand volunteers in camp at Raleigh were greatly moved by the sad event. The Raleigh papers of the 13th, contained the following:

"At Camp Grimes the soldier blood boiled with hatred for the nation that had done the bloody deed, and 'to the front' became the watchword.

"'I hope it's true,' said a member of the Governor's Guard, 'that we are to be sent at once to Cuba. We now have a mission—something to fight for—Worth Bagley's death must and shall be avenged.'

"Maj. E. M. Hayes, U. S. A.: 'That is terrible news. And Ensign Bagley had such a brilliant future before him. Even at this time he was the best known man of his rank in the United States Navy. I consider his death a national loss. Though I have met him but a few times, I was very much impressed with his manner and bearing. I have always watched his career with positive pleasure.'

"Col. Wm. H. S. Burgwyn, Colonel of the Second Regiment, South Carolina Volunteers: 'It is truly an extraordinary coincidence that North Carolina should lose the first soldier in 1861, and now the first in the present war. North Carolina has just given her brightest and best. She will demand back from Spain a like return, with tenfold increase. She has something now to fight for, and she will make as good a record in this war as she did in the last.'

"Col. A. D. Cowles, Adjutant General of North Carolina: 'The North Carolinians will remember the 'Maine' and they will remember, too, poor Bagley. Gallantly fighting for his country, he fell the first martyr in the cause of humanity. He poured out his heart's blood at the base of the standard on which the starry emblem of liberty proudly floated, and stricken unto death, a patriot's loving hope led his palsied arms to its fond embrace. As the angels kissed his eyelids down in sleep, lovingly he gazed upon the flag above him, and as the last faint whisper lingered on his stricken lips, he murmured: 'Mother and My Country.' Passing to fame's eternal camping ground, he saluted our banner in the sky and amid the glories of its folds, his soldier spirit was wafted to its God. 'Remember thee! aye, brave soldier, while memory holds a place in this distracted globe.' Remember thee! Yea, we'll remember the 'Maine' and you.'"

These expressions of sympathy came not only from the warlike living among arms in the white tented city of Camp Grimes. They came from all organizations, from all creeds, from all classes, from all colors. At each of the schools the children were gathered together, and the heroic manner of his death was told and his noble character portrayed. At the Centennial Graded School, of which Ensign Bagley had been a pupil, Mrs. Barbee, who had been his teacher, and Miss Mabel Hale, principal of the school, gave incidents in his life, and Superintendent Logan D. Howell spoke at length upon his career.

At Morson & Denson's school, where he was prepared for college, the present and former students, resolved to attend the funeral in a body, and appointed a committee of his class-mates, composed of Hubert A. Royster, William B. Snow, C. Van Fleming and W. W. Vass, to draw up appropriate resolutions. "We deeply mourn" said the former fellow students, "the end of a career so full of promise and the loss of one so rich in the noblest qualities of mind and character, yet we glory in the proud example of a life devoted to duty, filled with unselfish heroism, and fearlessly offered up in his country's cause."

The news came during the commencement of Shaw University, the chief Baptist school for the education of the colored youth in the State. President Meserve announced the death, and resolutions drawn by a committee composed of A. B. Vincent, E. A. Johnson, J. A. Dodson and Chas. F. Meserve, were adopted. Rev. John E. White, who was delivering the address, said "the death of Ensign Bagley was the first contribution of American blood to the cause of liberty in Cuba," and the audience was melted to tears as he spoke of his noble life and heroic death.

The L. O'B Branch Camp No. 515, United Confederate Veterans, (A. B. Stronach, Commander and J. C. Birdsong, Adjutant,) resolved to attend the funeral in a body, and appointed a committee composed of J. M. Monie, A. M. Powell and A. B. Stronach to draft resolutions, from which the following is taken:

"North Carolina is again called upon to lose one of her beloved sons. By sea and land her sons have made glorious history of this great commonwealth. In the pages of history the young hero of Cardenas will take his place in that proud galaxy of names which have immortalized their country.

"See him at duty's call, as he stands amid the shower of death-dealing missiles (fresh and ruddy as David, the shepherd boy), in the prime of his manly beauty, the embodiment of a line of heroes which North Carolina cherishes as her richest treasures. Never had mother nobler son. In him all that was pure and lofty in purpose found lodgment. Dignified without presumption, affable without familiarity, he united all graces that made him the idol of his friends and of his sailors. The perspective of the glories of a liberated Cuba did not intoxicate him, neither did the cloud of adversity, that so rapidly passed over him, serve to depress him. With a smile upon his face, with the flag of his country in his hand, with thoughts of loved ones at home, his face to the foe—thus passed away Ensign Worth Bagley.

"As if the soul that moment caught
Some treasure it through life had sought."

The Meade Post, No. 39, G. A. R., of Raleigh, vied with the L. O'B. Branch camp of Confederate Veterans in honoring the dead Ensign, and on the day of the funeral they marched together to Oakwood cemetery. On Memorial day, May 30th, a committee from the G. A. R. Camp composed of S. D. Wait, chairman, C. H. Beine and A. W. Shaffer, arranged for placing the floral contribution of Gen. Meade Post, No. 1, Dept. of Pennsylvania, on the grave of Ensign Bagley.

Memorial day exercises in Raleigh, May 30th, 1898, made new history in the re-uniting of the blue and gray. Just as the women and girls had decorated the graves of the Federal soldiers who sleep their last sleep in the National cemetery, a storm drove the assembled company to a sheltered place to hear the address. They hurried to the Confederate Home nearby and in the chapel of the Home, with the old Confederate veterans composing most of the audience, the exercises took place. The account in the Raleigh papers is thus condensed:

"It was an object lesson in the reuniting of the blue and the gray, such as perhaps has never before been witnessed in the whole country. It is certain that never in North Carolina were the blue and the gray so brought together. It was a sight not soon to be forgotten, the Federal soldier, speaking of the Southern valor in a Confederate chapel, and the eyes of Confederate soldiers moistened with tears at the speaker's reference to the young North Carolina hero, whose blood has forever banished sectionalism."

"President Chas, F. Meserve, of Shaw University, delivered the memorial oration. He said the South vies with the North in patriotic ardor and is pouring out her best life-blood in this struggle. After referring to the sublime spectacle of Gen. Lee, (with a grandson of Gen. Grant and a son of Benjamin Harrison on his staff,) and Gen. Wheeler, closing their military careers in uniform of the army of the United States, he said:

"But the greatest honor that could come to any State has come to liberty-loving North Carolina, where the memories of the Revolution are still alive and the spirit of Henry Clay still lingers. I say honor. It was indeed a great honor, but a most terrible sacrifice, and it touched deeply the heart of the nation, and the grief was felt by all. When Ensign Worth Bagley, shattered by a Spanish shell, grasped, as he fell upon the deck of the Winslow, the staff from which 'Old Glory' proudly waved, and, as his life-blood ebbed away, murmured, 'Mother and Country,' the South showed her loyal devotion to the Union and her fixed determination to maintain its integrity.

"The Southland has given up her fairest, her choicest and her best, and has made the first sacrifice in the cause of freedom for Cuba. The North mourns and weeps with her sister South in her sorrow. Sorrow has brought both sections close together, and shoulder to shoulder they will work out the destiny of the American republic."

"Miss Minnie May Curtis then read a beautiful original poem, from which the following verses are taken :

The North and South clasped hands above the first brave martyr's bier;
They both could claim him,—Pilgrim blood was blent with Chevalier !
Such fine commingling forces met to knit that sturdy frame,
To mould that brave heroic soul, who won a deathless name !

" The love of Freedom that beat strong within that Pilgrim sire,
Throbbed in this true young patriot breast with pure and holy fire,
And nerved his hand to do its best for crushed humanity,
To right a cruel, grievous wrong, and set a people free.

United now as ne'er before, a Nation mourns to-day,
For 'neath "Old Glory," sleeps the son of one who wore the gray,
So loving, gentle, faithful, good ; so strong, so brave, so true,
America may well rejoice in noble sons like you !

"The procession then moved to Oakwood cemetery, where the whole company stood with uncovered heads while Governor Russell and Mayor Russ and the Commander of the G. A. R. placed at the head of the grave of Ensign Worth Bagley the beautiful floral offering sent by the Meade G. A. R. Post of Philadelphia. The grave had already been literally covered with a profusion of flowers of the season, and was an embowered bank of the rarest and loveliest flowers, tastefully arranged by Steinmetz by order of the New York World, which paid this tribute to the memory of the first American officer to fall for Old Glory in this struggle. Above the bower of flowers, which were intertwined with laurel, were branched the pine and the palm, typifying the uniting of the North and the South over the grave of the Federal officer, son of a Confederate soldier. There were other beautiful tributes, among them one from the Loyal Legion of Women of Washington, D. C., and Ensign Alfred McKelthan, a class-mate of Ensign Worth Bagley at the Naval Academy. The company gathered about the grave, added choice flowers to the lovely decorations, and the choir sang "America." The clouds had passed away, and the last rays of the setting sun fell on the heads of the company as Rev. Dr. Curtis offered prayer, and Rev. Dr. Pittinger pronounced the benediction."

Seaton Gales Lodge, No. 64, I. O. O. F., passed resolutions saying that the Lodge " which was honored by having upon its roll the name of the father of the young and noble son, doth hereby extend to the grief stricken family the profound sympathy and condolence that the ties of fraternal love and esteem so forcefully

THE CLASS OF 1895 IN WHICH HE GRADUATED.
(BAGLEY ON TOP ROW AGAINST POST ON EXTREME LEFT.)

suggest." They were signed by B. H. Woodell and Henry J. Young, committee; E. G. Faust, Noble Grand, and Phil. Thiem, recording secretary.

At a meeting of the Board of Alderman of the city of Raleigh, Mayor Russ appointed Messrs. John C. Drewry, chairman; W. W. Parrish, and J. E. Hamlin a committee to draft resolutions, from which these extracts are taken:

"That we lament the untimely death of this gallant young officer, whose constant courage and devotion to duty has honored the city of his birth, and who has found the immortality that comes to a brave and noble soul who yields his life to the service of his country.

"Resolved, That as a child and boy and man the people of Raleigh have known and loved him, living as he did a life without fear and without reproach, and they will keep ever fresh in their hearts the precious memory of his life and virtues."

On the 20th of May, the anniversary of the Mecklenburg Declaration of Independence, in presenting a flag given by the ladies of Raleigh to the Governor's Guards, Capt. C. B. Denson made this reference to Ensign Bagley:

"And when you strike, remember that the first hero of this war to give his blood for his country, was your own friend and fellow-townsman, your schoolmate and fellow-Carolinian, now no longer our own, but blazoned by the triumph of fame around the world, as his great country's son."

## CHAPTER X.

### TRIBUTES FROM ARMY AND NAVY FRIENDS.

WHEREVER he went Worth Bagley made many friends. As a boy, he was popular with old and young. As a naval cadet, he won the love of his fellows, the confidence of his instructors, and the respect of his superior officers—one friend writing ' a history of the past few years of his life will be found inextricably woven in that of the Naval Academy, for he was of the kind that made history of the place in which he happened to be." In the discharge of his duties as an officer of the navy he not only came to number his fellow officers as his friends, but in every port in which his ship touched the charm of his attractive personality made him a host of friends. From all quarters have come words of sympathy to his stricken mother, evidencing that whether on shipboard, in places of danger, in the brilliant gatherings of the great cities and resorts in the quiet of vacation, in the school room, in the workshop, on the athletic field, everywhere, he showed the grace, strength and true chivalry that made men and women love to call him friend. The letters which hundreds of these friends have written to the darkened home of which he was the light are full of proofs of the strong hold he had upon the affections of those who had come into near relationship with him. The limits of this volume permit extracts only from a few who had known him intimately at the Naval Academy or afterward when he was an officer in the navy.

The tribute paid to him by Major General J. C. Breckinridge, the father of Ensign Bagley's room-mate at Annapolis and his most intimate friend, is as follows :

### " WAR'S TRIBUTE PAID."

" Ensign Bagley has given a name to our national annals which has a ring of sweetness and pathos in it like monastery bells, but all must mourn at the sacrifice of the individual, even though devoted to the cause of humanity. The charm of his character and his loyal reliability were tempered with such winning manners and sturdy strength that his exit from our sphere in the first flush and beauty of manhood makes the music cease while a wail is heard. Possibly the tragic death of no other young man of his age would have thrilled so many hearts with pain nor awakened so many to sympathy, especially in the sister services. That poets have sung to the theme of this gallant young life and noble death; that youth throughout the land have felt their hearts beat higher as they chose him for a model; that young and old, the daring and the fair, join in his praises and mourn for his loss is as natural as that honey should be produced from the dewy flower. It was the very nature of this young man to be loved and to win unstinted praise from all and for all that he did better than any one else could do. He was accustomed to have breathless thousands wait and watch what he, all unperturbed, would do next and do supremely well.

" He was my dead son's room-mate. They have been in my house like twin gods, endeared to all. I believe you will pardon me more emotion than can be properly expressed when in the midst of this campaign we stop to recall the loss our country's cause has brought to you and us. The State where he was born, the people he has served, the home so shattered can well hold his memory dear : he deserved well of his people.

" With admiration and affection for the dead and sincerest sympathy for the living, I remain, most sincerely yours,

"J. C. BRECKINRIDGE.

" Tampa, Fla."

Extracts from the letters of Ensign Bagley have already shown the friendship existing between him and Ensign Barnes, of Oklahoma. Before the death of Ensign Breckinridge the three were inseparable. After that mutual sorrow the friendship of these two young officers was strengthened by their common grief. Writing from " U. S. S. Vicksburg," off Havana, Cuba, to the mother of his dead friend, Ensign Barnes says :

When Worth died for his country's cause before Cardenas I lost as true a friend as God gives to a man and one whom I shall mourn the remainder of my life, for there is no one to take his place, to be the friend and companion he was to me.

"Please accept my tearful and heartfelt sympathy, for knowing him as I did to be the truest gentleman and noblest friend I also know what a son he was to you.

"Deprived of Bagley and Breckenridge in three short months I do not know what I shall do.

"For me they were the embodiment of chivalry and honor and I will miss them all my life.

"It seems as though I had lost myself, so completely do I grieve. To you and his sisters my heart goes out, feeling the anguish of the loss of a brother as you do that of a son. He lived ten days ago when I saw him last and walked down to the boat with my arm around his dear broad shoulders. My Dear Madam, I can write no more, please accept the sympathy I feel for that I would express. I too am bereaved."

Writing to a relative of his dead friend, Ensign Barnes says :

" There are true men in the world, but one does not often know and prove them. Worth Bagley's life was a short but unmistakable proof of a noble manhood, a deep-rooted character of gentle chivalry and sterling nobility. He died as a brave man would wish to die—in the midst of a well fought fight, battling for humanity's cause, front to the foe "

Ensign Alfred McKethan, of Fayetteville, N. C., who entered the Naval Academy on the same day that Ensign Bagley entered, and who was always one of his best friends, writes from " U. S. S. Solace " at Key West :

"The sad news of Worth's death was received on the 17th at sea from the dispatch boat. Sorry and sad am I......On account of the brotherly affection that has always existed between us, I feel his loss more than words can express. A friendship and affection from boyhood when we first started North in 1889, increased and strengthened as each day passed, until at last we were as brothers, and now as I look back upon a friendship never once marred by an unpleasant incident or word between us, my heart bleeds with sorrow and sadness to know that he has passed away. He gave his life to his country and died in its defense at his post of duty."

Paymaster Walter B. Izard, a classmate at Annapolis and a member of " the famous eleven " who defeated the West Point football team, writing from the " U. S. S. Machias," at Key West, says :

"I want to express my deepest sympathy for you at the loss of your noble son. I had known Worth so long and intimately that it seems hard to realize that so true an officer should be taken from us.

"I was ordered by the Department to accompany his body North, but as we have only just returned from Cardenas I did not receive the orders. I would like to have done something for him at the last."

Ensign R. Z. Johnston, of Lincolnton, N. C., a classmate and friend, writing from the " U. S. S. Oregon," says :

"When I heard the news we were in quarantine at Barbadoes. Some one rowing around the ship was asked the news and replied, 'Winslow sunk, Bagley killed.' It affected me strangely for I was terribly mad..... I liked and admired Worth very much, and you know that he loved his mother, which I think is the noblest trait in any man. We are all proud of him and very sorry for his mother whom he loved so dearly and who always came first in his thoughts."

Naval Constructor Homer L. Ferguson, of Waynesville, N. C., writing from his station on the Pacific, says :

"I am glad that the Old North State is to so fitly honor one of the bravest, noblest sons she ever had."

Ensign Harris Lanning, now of the training-ship Mohican, upon learning of the death of Ensign Bagley, upon his arrival from Honolulu, said to a reporter of the San Francisco Chronicle :

"I saw Bagley last only a few months ago, when, after two years cruising, we met at the Naval Academy to take our final examinations and receive our commissions. Bagley was known among his fellows as a man who knew not what fear was. For his bravery and good fellowship he was especially beloved by us all."

Charles F. McNeill, Galveston, Texas, writes :

" Worth and I were classmates at the Naval Academy in 1889-90 and our friendship was never broken until his tragic death.    *    *    * I am deeply grieved—for I have lost a friend."

Ensign A. H. A. Davis, U. S. Navy, of Louisburg, N. C., telegraphed from Tortugas :

" Please express my sorrow and deepest sympathy. We have lost a noble fellow."

Ensign Amon Bronson, U. S. Navy, telegraphed :

" To the memory of the best fellow I ever knew."

John William Wilen, cadet U. S. Military Academy, West Point, writes :

" I knew Worth when he was a cadet at Annapolis, and it is useless for me to speak of his many noble qualities of which we all know. I hope you may find comfort in knowing that he gave up his life as only a brave man can for his glorious flag."

Lieutenant Lawrence S. Adams, U. S. Navy, who attended the funeral at Raleigh, writes:

"As a friend of your son's, I want to express my sincere sympathy with you in your great loss, and also to express my personal regret in losing so good a friend."

Robert Coleman Bagby, Newport News, Va., writes:

"Your son was my good friend—a fine, noble fellow, possessing all the qualities that constitute an ideal naval officer. For two years I was associated with him at Annapolis, and it was there that I first knew him and learned to admire him. * * * Every cadet that knew him admired him. I have followed his career with the greatest interest. His death came to me as an awful shock, and his loss is a personal one."

Mr. Wm. J. Reecke, of St. James, Mo., a former classmate at the Naval Academy, in a St. Louis paper, says:

"In all the various duties and activities at the Naval Academy in which manliness and true courage make up the record of a man's efficiency, Worth Bagley was in the foremost rank of the leaders. Personally, his cheerful disposition and earnest endeavor to do his duty earned the good will and respect of every officer and cadet at the Naval Academy. The country has lost one of its brightest officers."

Prof. Samuel Garner, of the Naval Academy faculty, writes:

"Ensign Bagley was strongly imbued with a sense of duty. When once he had conceived anything as a duty, he immediately sought to put his whole energy into it, firmly resolved to succeed at any cost. This earnestness of purpose Bagley carried into the athletic sports in which he engaged and to it was attributable his wonderful success as a 'footballist'......In the class room Cadet Bagley was a model young man--deferential and respectful to his instructors, in a word, a perfect gentleman in his demeanor—always in earnest, always attentive to the matter in hand. I do not recall a single instance on his part where he failed to fairly prepare his lesson, how many soever other claims there may have been upon his time. Here, as elsewhere, his earnest nature would not allow him to neglect a palpable duty. In these respects I feel sure that the testimony of his other instructors would follow along the same lines as my own."

Rev. Robert H. Williams, who was pastor of the Presbyterian Church at Annapolis while he was a cadet, writes:

"Permit me, who had an interest in your son, Worth, long before this war commenced, to offer a word or two of sympathy. As pastor of the Presbyterian Church, of Annapolis, for nearly ten years, a large number of cadets of the Naval Academy came under my pastoral care, and your son among them. I remember your son with a great deal of interest and pleasure. He was a general favorite and bade fair to be very efficient as an officer, and very useful to the missionary in the foreign countries he might visit."

Among his classmates and friends at the Naval Academy to whom he was deeply attached, was Ensign Merritt, who perished on the Maine. Mr. W. W. Merritt, of Red Oak, Iowa, father of Ensign Merritt, writes :

"My heart goes out in sympathy to you in this great sorrow that has come to you. Your noble son and my son were classmates and intimate friends. I have often heard him speak of your son in terms of admiration and affection. My son was foully murdered in the harbor of Havana. Your son had occasion to 'remember the Maine' and doubtless controlled by an almost uncontrollable impulse he braved danger on that fatal day at Cardenas harbor. May we not hope that they, with that other classmate, Breckinridge, are now together on the other shore beyond war's alarms."

A sister of Lieut. Jenkins, who was lost on the Maine, writes :

"Although a stranger, I do not feel you will deem these few lines an intrusion, for none I am sure can feel more profound sympathy for you in the loss of your dear boy than do the mother and sister of ours. Aside from the common bond of sympathy existing I feel that the life of your noble son was given partly in avenging the death of my brother and I assure you my whole heart goes out to you in your sorrow."

Dr. Paul J. Dashiell, an instructor at the Naval Academy, writes :

"I saw a great deal of Bagley, in athletics specially, and his genial ways and sharp plucky play and coolness under trying circumstances left a name here that none has eclipsed......All liked him--men and women--and personally I was much attached to him......His athletic achievements which will live very long here rather reached a climax in the very difficult goal he kicked in '93 against West Point, thus winning the game for the navy."

Mrs. Robley D. Evans, wife of the Commander of the Iowa, writes :

"We were first drawn to your son by his rare personal beauty and charm of manner six years ago at the Naval Academy, and as he matured and developed his nature and character seemed to deepen and sweeten until he promised a very high and noble future to us who watched him.

"I saw him last at Key West in the middle of March, about two months ago, and my husband and I were much impressed by the splendid development that had come to him. He always bore himself in a princely way, and two months ago there was added to that bearing a strength and sweetness and power of expression that gave his fine face an almost seraphic expression. His deep suffering, which we shared, in the loss of his friend, Cabell Breckinridge, I think had elevated, fortified his own spirit. In writing you this I am sure that Captain Evans would agree with all I say for he loved and valued your son, as we all did and do, and always shall do while memory lasts.

"When your deep anguish shall have become a part of your life—for that is all we mothers can expect when such a blow falls upon us—you will realize that your boy died as he would have wished, in the flush and stir of battle, with no lingering or time for pain.

"'He flashed his soul out with the guns,
And took his haven at once.'

"My only boy, who loved yours, sailed for Havana yesterday afternoon on the Massachusetts, so you can understand that I know how to feel for you with very tender sympathy."

Mrs. Priscilla Alden Nicholson, whose husband had been his instructor and superior officer, writes:

"In the sad death of your brave son I feel, as an old friend of his, I must offer my deepest sympathy. In our life in the navy we are as one, so united, and my heart is all interest for those in such dreadful peril as the present.

"While at the Academy my late husband instructed your son, and always admired him as a sterling youth, and while on the U. S. S. Montgomery found him a fine officer. He was in charge of his battery, and spoke of him always in the highest terms of praise. Last June, when taking his final examinations, he was a great deal at our house, and only last December passed Sunday as my guest. I have always felt I knew him well, and trust you will believe how deeply I mourn with you and yours. Please accept my sincerest sympathy—words fail me.  *  *  *  He died bravely—doing his duty faithfully to the end—but it seems a sacrifice of a much-needed life."

Lieut. Jos. B. Batchelor, Jr., U. S. A., Fort Slocum, New York, a native of Raleigh, N. C., writes:

"His work was well done—all, from first to last, well done! On the edge of the strife, whose course no eye can foresee, all eyes may see that the sacrifice offered is of our very best. Had he lived, high honor must have come to him, and we his comrades, afloat and ashore, mourn the loss of the deeds he would have done; but who shall say that the fresh young life so gallantly given to his country, instantly on demand, is not of more worth than all the long triumph of a life time......I am serving here with many who knew him well. Of him no word is spoken save in praise. All speak of him, and speak such words as any mother would be proud to hear."

The wife of an officer at the Naval Academy, writes:

"We knew your dear son very well, and both my husband and I were devoted to him. There never has been a cadet more universally loved and admired here, and it must be some comfort to you to know he died doing his duty unflinchingly and leaving an unspotted record behind him."

Mrs Wm H. G. Bullard, writing for herself and her husband, who was instructor in Physics and Chemistry at the Naval Academy and who is now on the "U. S. S. Columbia," writes:

"We were both devoted to Worth Bagley and all of his first class year he was most constantly at our quarters, and if he had been one of my own family I could not have felt his loss more deeply. A sweeter, gentler and more refined nature I never saw."

Closing its account of the disaster at Cardenas, the Army and Navy Journal, says:

"Ensign Bagley was a great favorite in navy circles."

## CHAPTER XI.

### PUBLIC TRIBUTES

IN many public gatherings throughout the country the heroism of Ensign Bagley was the subject of eloquent orators, who found in his death the theme for inculcating patriotism and those virtues that make the highest type of manhood Only a few can be given here. Concluding a noble speech, to the Kentucky volunteers in camp at Lexington, with a prayer for his own boys who were in the ranks, Henry Watterson said:

"In that prayer let me include each and every one of you, though I would rather see my boys, and each and every one of you, lying by the side of that brave and lovely sailor lad wi om North Carolina has just given up as Heaven's first sacrifice upon the altars of the nation and mankind, than that one feather should be plucked from the eagle's wing, or a syllable of reproach be justly cast upon the name and fame of our dear Kentucky."

At the commencement exercises of the University of North Carolina, May 29th, June 1st, inclusive, both the preacher and the orator paid eloquent tributes to the memory of Ensign Bagley. It was fitting that the institution in which he had passed the entrance examinations, before receiving his appointment to Annapolis, should feel a special pride in his glory. In the course of the baccalaureate sermon on "Perfect Manhood" from Ephesians 4:13, by Rev. Wilbur F. Tillett, D. D., Dean of the Theological Faculty of the Vanderbilt University, he said:

"The whole American nation is now watering with its tears the new made grave in your Capitol City where Ensign Worth Bagley has been laid to rest. If a Greek historian were to record how that brave boy, with the blood of a noble and honored Carolina ancestry in his veins, went in obedience to superior orders to the place of danger on the ill-fated Winslow, and gave up his pure young life in gallant defense of his country's flag as it sought to carry freedom to the downtrodden and oppressed, can we be in doubt for a moment as to which of

TEACHING WIG WAG CODE OF SIGNALS ON THE MAINE.
(BAGLEY OFFICER ON THE RIGHT WITH FLAG.)

these two words the historian would choose in calling him a MAN........
Brave boy, thou art not dead ; thou hast simply taken thy well earned place alongside the gallant ANDRES of never dying Thermopylæ and among the noble young heroes of our Anglo-Saxon race whose names will find an abiding place in the memorabilia of ideal manhood and the history of the State that loved you in life and now honors you in death."

Hon. Hannis Taylor, of Mobile, Ala., Minister to Spain from 1893 to 1897, in the course of his address at the University on " Our Widening Destiny," made the following reference to Ensign Bagley :

" By some strange fatality the sons of this State seem to be called first when such an oblation is to be made. In that dreadful moment when the North and South were about to be torn apart, North Carolina, a border State, who loved the Union as she loved her life, held out her pleading hands to her brethren on either side in the hope that by kind and tender words she could put away wrath and avert the impending strife. Not until her most strenuous efforts had failed ; not until she had been cruelly maligned and misunderstood did she finally resolve to enter into that prolonged and bloody conflict to which she contributed the first victim in the person of Henry Wyatt, who fell at the battle of Bethel, on the soil of Virginia. May it not have been that North Carolina, through her heroic though unavailing efforts to avert the civil war and save the Union, won for herself the post of honor when the time came for the first victim to be offered up upon the altar of the united nation in its first war against a foreign foe ? In a proud, yet stricken spirit, we can all feel that the victim was worthy of the sacrifice. When the brave and pure young life of Worth Bagley went out on the tide at Cardenas we yielded up one worthy of a race of heroic men. Of such a life and such a death, typical as it was of a great national event, there should be some permanent memorial. We owe it to ourselves to perpetuate in bronze or marble the memory not only of our heroic son, but of the noble mother who gave him to his country.

" If we can do no more let us fix a tablet upon the walls of the capitol at Raleigh, and carve upon it the fateful words from his last letter in which he told her : " You have enough of the Spartan in you, if you wish, to say, ' With your shield or upon it,' and that is what you must always say to me." Such words have an eternal meaning coming as they did from one who was about to die. Let us hang them up for monuments so that the generations yet to come may know that

" At the altar of their nation,
Stood that mother and her son,
He, the victim of oblation;
Panting for his immolation;
She, in priestess' holy station,
Weeping words of consecration,
While God smiled his approbation,
Blessed the boy's self-abnegation,
Cheered the mother's desolation,
When the sacrifice was done."

In his commencement oration at Davidson College, Hon. Theo. F. Kluttz, of Salisbury, said :

"Now that the silver bells of Peace have been silenced by the dread sounds of War, North Carolina is again giving freely of her best and bravest to her country's cause. As at Bethel, she gave in WYATT, the first martyr to the vain but glorious struggle for Southern independence ; so now, at Cardenas, she gives the first martyr in this war for Humanity; nor could she have offered a more costly oblation than the brave young life of gallant WORTH BAGLEY.

"I knew him well : a gallant, manly fellow, the pride and idol of a widowed mother's heart: capable, brilliant, enthusiastic, ambitious, loving and loved--with everything in life to live for, he yet laid down his life bravely, willingly, for his country's honor, and in the great cause of humanity.

"His name can never die.

"Let it live in story and in song, in marble and in bronze, as long as patriotism has a votary, or heroism a shrine."

Hon. Hugh G. Miller, of Norfolk, Va., who delivered the commencement oration at Elon College, thus alluded to Ensign Bagley's death :

"And this evening I bow my head with a feeling of reverence almost akin to consecration as I stand upon the sacred soil that gave Ensign Worth Bagley to this Union, the first American to give up his life for his country in the Spanish-American war. And when at last over the ruins of Morro Castle the 'Lone Star of the Pearl of the Antilles' shall float and glitter side by side with our stars and stripes, the world will remember that it was the life blood of a Carolinian that first consecrated the divine cause of Cuban Liberty."

Rev. Joseph F. Berry, Fraternal delegate to the General Conference of the M. E. Church, South, at Baltimore, May 18th, in his address, said :

"A nation's tears have fallen upon the bier of Ensign Bagley, and a nation has remembered that the first American soldier to fall at his post, the stars and stripes waving about him, was a youthful son of North Carolina."

At the meeting of the North Carolina Colonial Dames, held in Wilmington, May 25th, resolutions were passed, and in an address, the President, Mrs. Geo. W. Kidder, made this reference to Ensign Bagley:

"If the deeds of valor of a dead and gone generation appeal to us, how much more are we thrilled by the daring and courage of the men of our own day, with whom we are in touch either by word, thought, or kindred ties. Foremost among them is North Carolina's brave young Ensign—foremost because he was the first martyr, and as such will go down conspicuously into history.

"He ventured love and life and youth
For the great prize of death in battle."

"'One touch of nature makes the whole world akin,'" and the law of universal motherhood makes us—a body of patriotic women—claim this young hero as our own and calls forth a tender and hearty response to the appeal for a monument to his memory."

The following resolution, suggested by General W. P Roberts, and introduced by Professor E. E. Britton, was adopted by a rising vote of the Democratic State Convention, held in Raleigh May 26th:

"Resolved, That as Carolinians, proud at all times of the honors, the achievements and patriotic sacrifices of the sons of our beloved State, we proclaim our admiration of the heroic conduct of Ensign Worth Bagley, of the United States Navy, which caused a sacrifice of his young and promising life in his country's cause, and we extend to his noble mother our sympathy in the anguish she has been called upon to suffer in the death of her noble and heroic boy—now the nation's son."

The platform, Ohio Republican State Convention, in session at Columbus, June 22d, contained these words:

"To the friends and relatives of Ensign Bagley, whose noble young life was the first forfeit of the war, we send condolence."

The Indiana State Democratic Convention in its platform, "rejoices in the heroic deeds of Dewey, Bagley and Hobson."

In a debate in the House of Representatives on the first of June, Hon. R. Z. Linney, of the Eighth North Carolina District, said:

"The State of North Carolina always does its full duty, in time of war or in time of peace. She not only furnishes troops, but she furnishes the best troops in the world. The first soldier who gave up his life in the late war between the States was a North Carolinian. The first who shed his blood in the war with Spain was a North Carolinian. And such was also the case in the war of the Revolution. Let me call attention to the sacrifice that State has recently made.

"Worth Bagley stood amid the fire-flames of war at a period that tried men's souls; and amid the volleys of shot and canister from the strongholds of the enemy he had the cool, philosophic courage to utter expressions that none but the noblest heroes of the world could have uttered: 'Throw me a rope! Heave the ship, boys! It is too warm for comfort here!' One moment afterwards off went the head of one of the grandest patriots and noblest soldiers of the United States [Applause.]

"The services of the citizen soldiery of North Carolina will place her standing as a State up to high-water mark. The example of Worth Bagley is the standard my State has set for courage and devotion to principle. We simply invite other States to come up to that standard. I have no doubt all the soldiers of all the States of the Union, from Mississippi to the State of my friend from Washington, will do all they can to come up to the high standard of Worth Bagley."

Mrs. Flora Adams Darling, A. M., President of the Daughters of the Revolution, in a letter to Mrs. Spier Whitaker, Regent for North Carolina, conveyed in loving words the sympathy of the patriotic societies.

Mrs. Alice McL. Birney sent the sympathy of the National Congress of Mothers.

At the hour of the funeral service in Raleigh, May 16th business was suspended in the town of Plymouth, N. C., and services were held in the courthouse and bells were tolled. Mayor Blount presided, and addresses were made by Rev. E. P. Green, Rev. D. W. Davis, Rev. G. L. Finch and Mr. H. S. Ward. "The Roanoke Riflemen, Company E, attended in a body, with crape bands around their arms; the drums were wrapped in mourning, and the muffled beat of the dead march added solemnity to the occasion," says the Roanoke Beacon.

Rev. A. W. Cheatham, rector of Trinity Church, Nashville, Tenn., held memorial services in his church on the 15th of May, and delivered an appreciative eulogy.

Of the organizations sending resolutions of sympathy to the family in addition to those already referred to, were the Cape Fear Lodge No. 2, I. O. O. F., and Wilmington Lodge No. 139, I. O. O. F., of Wilmington; the New Jersey Society of the Daughters of the Revolution; the Women's National Relief Association; the General Secretary of the Daughters of the Revolution; the Woman's National Cuban League; the Texas Society of the Daughters of the American Revolution, and the North Carolina Society at Washington, D. C.

The Southwestern Presbyterian University, Clarkesville, Tenn., placed its flag at half-mast, and Chancellor Summey wrote that Worth Bagley's name was inscribed upon it. Many other like tributes were paid in memory by schools, colleges and communities.

On the day of the funeral in Raleigh by order of the Governor of Virginia the flags on the capitol at Richmond were placed at half mast.

The first resolutions passed by any military organization were passed by Company M, "The Queen City Guards" (Capt. H. S. Chadwick) in camp Bryan Grimes at Raleigh, on May 13th. Every member of that company contributed to the erection of a monument.

## CHAPTER XII.

### TRIBUTES FROM PUBLIC MEN.

"PRESIDENT McKINLEY deeply deplored the death of the gallant fellow. Both President McKinley and Secretary Long, in the expressions of their sorrow at the tragedy, and admiration for the conduct of the Winslow's crew, made it clear that the Winslow had acted under orders when she entered Cardenas harbor."

The New York Journal of May 14th contained the above telegram from Washington.

The papers have been full of tributes from eminent public men, and many of them have written words of sympathy to the mother of the brave boy who sleeps in his deathless grave at Oakwood. Room is made here only for a few of the personal letters and telegrams received by Mrs. Bagley from public men of other States than North Carolina.

Hon. John D. Long, Secretary of the Navy, wrote:

"WASHINGTON, D. C., May 17, 1898.

"My Dear Mrs. Bagley:

"I am in receipt to day of a letter from Rev. T. N. Haskell (copy of which is herein enclosed), requesting that I forward to you the attached verses on the death of your son.

"In forwarding you this, may I not be permitted also to offer you my heartfelt sympathy at your irreparable loss. Mr. Haskell's quotation of the letter from President Lincoln seems to me especially appropriate. You, too, have the thanks of the Republic, and a solemn pride in having 'laid so costly a sacrifice on the altar of freedom.'

"You also have the assurance that the whole navy mourns with you in the loss of your son, who died at his post, in the performance of a daring duty—one of the bravest of the brave.

"With great respect,
"Very sincerely yours,
"JOHN D. LONG."

"1651 EMERSON AVENUE,
"DENVER, COL., May 12, 1898.

"Dear Mr. Secretary Long:

"The news of Ensign Bagley's tragic death, with a sketch of his beautiful character and life and brave deeds, in the midst of which the bursting shell nearly beheaded him and killed four of the brave fellows by his side, has just come to my desk, and I could not refrain from impromptuing the enclosed poem for his deeply afflicted mother, whose address I cannot learn. On the back of the slip I have copied President Lincoln's pathetic letter to Widow Bixby, of Boston. I wish, even in the midst of your mighty deeds and duties now, you would see that the message is sent to that Jochebed, 'Glorious Mother,' as soon as may be. Worth Bagley's mother deserves well of all.

"T. N. HASKELL."

## LINCOLN'S LETTER OF CONDOLENCE TO A BEREFT WIDOW IN BOSTON,

November 21st, 1864.

My Dear Madam :

I have been shown in the files of the War Department, a statement of the Adjutant General of Massachusetts, that you are the mother of five sons who have died gloriously on the field of battle. I feel how weak and fruitless must be any word of mine, which should attempt to beguile you from the grief of a loss so overwhelming, but I cannot refrain from tendering to you the consolation that may be found in the thanks of the Republic they died to save. I pray that our Heavenly Father may assuage the anguish of your bereavement, and leave you only the cherished memory of the loved and lost, and the solemn pride that must be yours, to have laid so costly a sacrifice upon the altar of Freedom.

Yours very respectfully and sincerely,

ABRAHAM LINCOLN.

## ENSIGN BAGLEY AND HIS BOYS.

### BY T. N. HASKELL.

#### An Impromptu.

When Israel's "firstlings of the flock"
  (Upon Jehovah's altar laid)
Besprinkled blood upon the rock
  On which the offering was made.
When Ellsworth fell, a holocaust,
  And in the White House "lay in state,"
Mankind conceived how much it cost
  Humanity to liberate.

When Ensign Bagley fought and fell,
  As the first offering of this land—
The victim of that vicious shell
  Exploding 'mong his valiant band—
O, God! How great the human gift,
  A widow's son, so wise and pure,
The Spanish barbarism to lift
  And Cuban liberty secure.

(And must men fight and must men fall
  And give their lives for greatest good?
The few to fall for good of all,
  And broaden out our brotherhood?
This problem, like thy Providence,
  Seems awe-inspiring when'er seen,
And it must have long ages hence
  To learn much that its lessons mean.)

O, Widow Bagley! Could you see
  Your son's proud name—above all praise—
Emblazoned—as 'twill surely be—
  Down to his country's latest days.
You would thank God for such a son
  And that his death in such a scene,
Doth decorate all he hath done
  And show what Martyrdom doth mean.

"The Boys" that fell at Bagley's side,
  Be blazoned, too, in types of blood,
Proclaimed henceforth "their country's pride,"
  To make all boys both brave and good!
Their memory—and that of the "Maine"—
  Like "resurrection from the dead."
Shall give the world their lives again
  Whene'er their names are known or read.

Hon. W. J. Bryan, Lincoln, Neb.. "Relying for an excuse upon a brief but pleasant acquaintance with your son, I write to tender you my sympathy in your great bereavement, and at the same time to bid you find consolation in the thought that, while it is the lot of all to die, it is the good fortune of but few to meet so honorable a death as that which befell your boy. Time, that great healer of wounds, will assuage your grief, but it will only brighten the glory that crowns the memory of Worth Bagley."

Hon. Hoke Smith, Atlanta, Ga.: "I spent last week at Key West and was on the Winslow with Ensign Bagley. I was with him several hours. I am deeply grieved and sympathize with you with all my heart."

Hon. Clark Howell, Atlanta, Ga.: "Permit me to extend deep sympathy in the bereavement of Ensign Bagley's family. The fact that the blood of this brave young Southerner is the first shed on our side builds an everlasting monument to his memory and emphasizes more than anything else could have done the fact that this is a re-united country."

Senator Pritchard: "Permit me to tender you my sincere sympathy in this your hour of great bereavement."

President Geo. T. Winston, University of Texas: "My heart bleeds for you in your awful sorrow. May God strengthen and comfort you! Only a few months ago I saw him here on the Texas, so happy, so noble and handsome and so admired and beloved by all."

Senator Butler: "He died fighting under the stars and stripes in the cause of humanity and the advancement of republican institutions. His gallant life and heroic death will do honor to his State, and, indeed, to the whole country."

Booker T. Washington: "I feel it to be the duty of negro citizens as well as white citizens to contribute to erect a monument to the memory of Ensign Worth Bagley."

O'Brien Moore, Charleston, W. Va.: "I send congratulations. I would rather have a dead Bagley for a relative than a hundred ordinary live men."

Gen. W. R. Cox, Secretary of the U. S. Senate: "Not only individuals, but the nation laments the sacrifice. Your affliction is indeed grevious, but yet there is amidst the darkness a silver lining to the cloud, when we recall that at the command of his country he went promptly to the front, fell with his face to the country's foe, and parting left behind him a light that illumines his chosen profession."

Rev. Thomas Dixon Jr., New York : " Please express my heart's deepest sympathy in the great sorrow in the death of the young hero at Cardenas. I am proud of him as a North Carolinian. I am proud of him as a young Southerner. I am proud of him as an American. I thank God that he reserved for the defeated and poverty-stricken Southland the pain and glory of the first heroic sacrifice for the new nation that has entered upon the achievement of its divine destiny. ......The young hero's name is a household word in every nook and corner of America to-day."

Henry Jerome Stockard, Fredericksburg, Va.: "Life at longest is but a breath : whether we live a day or a century it makes no difference—there is no 'long,' no 'short' life when measured with the infinite reach of time and eternity : then that spirit which went out in the blinding, petrific shell at Cardenas went out in a veritable blaze of glory. The nation reveres him and will remember him."

## CHAPTER XIII.

### SEALED THE UNION WITH HIS BLOOD.

"WE are all Worth Bagley's countrymen" was the concluding sentence of an editorial in the New York Tribune referring to the death of the first American officer in the war with Spain, the son of an officer in the Confederate Army. The Tribune's editorial, reminding one of the utterances of Horace Greeley, ended with this paragraph :

"It is worth while also to remember that the South furnishes the first sacrifice of this war. Ensign Bagley was a native of North Carolina. With his blood he has sealed the union in arms of the North and South. A people who once fought against the Stars and Stripes send one of their sons as the first sacrifice for the honor and glory of that flag. There is no North and no South after that. We are all Worth Bagley's countrymen."

In the same spirit writes the Springfield Republican, voicing the breadth of patriotism breathed into it by Sam Bowles:

"The loss of life in the Cardenas engagement was our first sacrifice of the sort in this war. Let us not forget that the first American officer to die for his country was from the South. In view of the great and tragic past, this fact possesses an interest that touches the hearts of all Americans. In the red blood of the young Carolinian, the North and South have sealed their perpetual reconciliation."

FUNERAL SCENES AT RALEIGH.

LYING IN STATE AT STATE CAPITOL. VIEW FROM THE HEAD.
HONOR GUARD AT THE BAGLEY HOME.
FUNERAL SERVICES AND CORTEGE AT CAPITAL SQUARE.
FLOWER DECKED GRAVE, WITH GRANDFATHER'S GRAVE TO LEFT, FATHER'S TO THE RIGHT.
CAPITOL SQUARE DURING FUNERAL SERVICES.

From all sources have come similar expressions. The G. A. R. Posts and the Confederate Veteran Camps have sent resolutions and wreaths of flowers to place upon the grave. The most historic of the actions taken by any organization outside of North Carolina was by the George G. Meade Post No. 1 of Philadelphia, the oldest Grand Army organization in America. The Philadelphia Press thus tells of the method employed by the Meade post to do honor to Ensign Bagley:

"The handsome floral design which members of George G. Meade Post No. 1, Grand Army of the Republic, will lay on the new-made grave of Ensign Worth Bagley, the hero of Cardenas, was completed yesterday. To-morrow it will be sent to the Mayor of Raleigh, N. C., with the Post's expressions of sympathy and eulogies of the gallant conduct of the brave Southern boy who gave his life for the flag of a reunited nation.

"This pretty tribute by which gray Northern veterans will memorialize the bravery of a young Southern officer is touchingly symbolical of the sentiment that prompts its sending. It speaks tenderly of the past and hopefully of the future. On a large snow-white wreath of immortelles, significant of the undying fame of the Southern hero whose name it commemorates, lies a grim and heavy sword, crossed on its worn scabbard, and tied below to the wreath by broad strands of the national colors.

"The sword is a time and war worn weapon, knicked and blunt-pointed, rust-eaten and stained with blood that flowed a third of a century ago, frayed on its wire-bound hilt—mute testimony of deeds of valor in the thick of terrific slaughter. The symbolism is touching in its import. For this blood-cut sword is a relic of one of the fierce and deciding battles of the war between North and South. In hand-to-hand combat it was wrested from one of the boys in gray by one of the boys in blue, on the death-strewn field of Gettysburg. Long prized as a trophy won in chivalric combat, it is now the gift of a member of the first Grand Army Post of the country, the Post that bears the name of Meade, the hero of Gettysburg, as a tribute to the bravery of the South.

"Raised to strike at the nation, captured and shorn of power by a defender of the nation, at length returned in forgiveness to the Commonwealth that was foremost in the civil strife, it tells the whole story of a divided country reunited and devoted to a common flag.

"Further significant of the sentiment that prompts the sending of this tribute is the word "United" in purple immortelles, wrought prettily on the background of white, between the points of the sword and scabbard. On the ribbons of national colors that hold the sword and scabbard to the wreath loom, in gilt lettering the inscriptions:—

"Ensign Worth Bagley, U. S. N.
"George G. Meade Post, No. 1, G. A. R.,
Philadelphia."

"Veterans of Meade Post speak proudly of the act of chivalry toward the men of the Southland. Colonel William Harkness, Jr., who is a member of the Memorial Committee that sends the tribute, said: "We send this wreath to the people of the South as an outward expression of what all Northern soldiers feel toward their old foes of Dixie. We all harbor the kindliest feeling toward Southern soldiers. We want to forgive and forget. We want to wipe out all that bitter feeling of the past and we are glad to have this opportunity to show our sympathy in the loss of a son of the South and our admiration for a Southern officer's valor.

"We have long since come to believe that the boys in gray were sincere in their belief in the righteousness of their cause, and we respect them for their heroic devotion to principle. They were brave men and good fighters."

Accompanying this historic tribute was a tender letter of sympathy to the mother. Placed on the grave by Federal and Confederate soldiers, this wreath and sword will find a permanent place in the State Library at Raleigh, N. C., typifying the obliteration of sectionalism and proving that the long cherished hopes for a reunited country have been realized.

On May 30th, a beautiful wreath of red roses and ivy, with streamers of the national colors sent by the loyal legion of Women of Washington, D. C., was placed on the grave along with the tribute from Meade Post.

About the same time, the New York Chapter of the United Daughters of the Confederacy held a meeting and passed resolutions of sympathy. In forwarding the resolutions, Mrs. M. L. Brodnax, Corresponding Secretary, wrote to Mrs. Bagley:

"While every member feels tenderest emotions of pity for the mother, they rejoice with you in the glory and honor which will forever rest upon the memory of your son whose noble life was sacrificed for his country... At the memorial services the most beautiful tribute was paid to your gallant boy by the orator of the day. Allusion was made to the graves in our dear Southland, where the father and son lay side by side, heroes of the two wars, one in the blue the other in the gray, and the fact that the first blood that was poured out as a sacrifice was that of a Southerner, was recalled with great pride by the speaker."

In his Memorial day address in Philadelphia, Commander John W. Frazier, of the Col. Fred Taylor Post, in the course of a patriotic address on the sublime spectacle of hearing "the Union cheer and the Rebel yell mingling in melody," said:

"Can we do better upon this Memorial Day than to highly resolve that this re-united country of ours baptized with the blood of the martyred heroes of the Maine; cemented by the death of North Carolina's Bagley—the Ellsworth of the conflict—shall, under Divine guidance, have a new birth of Fraternity, Charity and Loyalty that the sectional animosities that have beset us for a generation shall be obliterated forever; that all enmity and prejudice between the North and the South shall be forever buried, and now that an indestructible Union binds us together in purpose and patriotism to make the fellowship cordial and sincere, as tender and lasting as a mother's love, respecting each other's sufferings and sorrows with American manhood and sympathy? It is our duty as past soldiers of the Republic, as American citizens, to help bring about these things."

When this Federal soldier was thus speaking of the reunited nation, the R. F. Webb Confederate Camp No. 818, of Durham, N. C. (Col. Julian S. Carr, Commander, and Capt. N. A. Ramsey Adjutant) in a series of resolutions said:

"The first blood that has been offered on the altar of humanity and in the cause of Cuba's freedom is full worth the sacrifice. The spirit of Worth Bagley has gone to join that of Henry Wyatt. Brave spirits both, with whom the post of danger was ever the post of honor, and whose bravery and gallantry have made richer the history of our common country."

Among many letters from Federal soldiers the following is given as showing the spirit of the men who followed Grant in the War Between the States:

AUBURN, N. Y., May 25th, 1898.

DEAR MADAM:—

Although a graduate of the prison pens of Petersburg and Libby, Va., and of Salisbury, N. C., and though my two visits to your beautiful city, as a prisoner of war, were made under painful conditions and circumstances, still, so great a healer is time, and so strong is love for one's country and its citizens, that I find myself among the thousands of others in our reunited land, dropping a tear over the sad fate of your noble boy who so recently gave up his life as a sacrifice in the cause of America and humanity.

While it is true that "one touch of nature makes the whole world kin" I believe it to be equally true that only those who have suffered greatly for country's sake can best sympathize with one another. It is with that feeling that I as a Union soldier of the late war, send to you as a widow of a Confederate soldier, my heart-felt sympathy as you sit by the new made grave of him who belonged to and died for neither the North nor the South, but the whole country united under one flag, and now more closely bound together in a bond of perfect union by the sacrifice of this young patriot's blood.

Respectfully,

ROBERT L. DRUMMOND.

Rev. James L. Tryon, rector of All Saints church, of Attleboro, Mass., on Sunday May 29th, preached a sermon before the Wm. A. Streeter Post, G. A. R., at a memorial service to the victims of the Maine, Private Wesley Brass, and Ensign Worth Bagley. At the request of Mr. Tryon, Mrs. Bagley sent flowers and a picture of her son. This extract is taken from the sermon:

"Worth Bagley was a young man characteristic of his time. Public-spirited, ambitious in the best sense, in mind thoroughly and conscientiously trained. An athlete of athletes, built like a Greek; a warrior of warriors, brave as a Spartan. The flower of the South; tender as gallant, in love of mother none surpassing, he was a gentleman like General Lee. He died as the Southern boy would pray to die; his last command the grace of knighthood, his arm around the one true flag."

In his memorial address at Arlington, Senator Thurston said:

"If I read God's history aright, civilization and Christianity have not come from the survival of the fittest, but by the sacrifice of the best. What puny human intelligence dares to assert that the blood of Lexington was not sacred, even as the blood of Calvary? Warren at Bunker Hill, Baker at Ball's Bluff, BAGLEY AT CARDENAS, all gloriously died to hasten the coming of God's kingdom on earth."

At Fredericksburg, Va., the Ladies Memorial Association placed a beautiful floral anchor beneath the shield of North Carolina on the Confederate monument, and attached to it was a card on which was written: "A memorial of the Courage and Faithfulness of Ensign Worth Bagley, another Laurel in North Carolina's Crown of Heroes. We place this tribute beneath her shield on our Confederate monument May 19th, 1898."

At Portsmouth, Va., on Confederate Memorial day, the most touching incident was the unfurling on the soldiers' and sailors' lot in the cemetery of a silken flag, inscribed to the memory of Ensign Worth Bagley, U. S. N., the first victim of the Spanish-American war. The walnut flagstaff was wound about with garlands. At the top was a chaplet of green and white, while around the base were grouped a profusion of floral designs and rare blossoms.

"We send this tribute of flowers in the name of Fraternity, Charity and Loyalty" were the closing words in a letter from the John Brady Woman's Relief Corps, auxiliary of the G. A. R. of Erie County Penn., in sending flowers that were placed on the grave by the side of the flowers sent by Confederate associations of Southern women—thus commingling the floral offerings of the noble women of the two sections who keep green the deeds of valor of the men who composed the armies of Lee and Grant.

From a mass of like clippings from editorial utterances of leading papers in every state in the Union, the following fairly represent the view the papers take of the heroic death of the young officer:

Hartford (Conn.) Courant: "All of us are proud of Worth Bagley, and his fame belongs to us all . All the states should be represented in the Monument Fund, and those New England States among the earliest. North Carolina was one of the Old Thirteen, and this is now—God be thanked for it!—a re-united country."

Washington (D. C.) Times: "It is fitting that the grave of the young Ensign should be marked by a monument erected by the North and South together The South is proud that Ensign Bagley was a North Carolina man; the North is proud that he was an American; and both should hasten to do him honor in the only way that remains."

Philadelphia Record : " The spirit that blossoms forth in such a tribute as that sent to Raleigh, N. C., to be laid on the grave of Ensign Bagley, honors the Grand Army even as it honors the immortal dead ; and its manifestation at this time is a proof that the lesson of decoration day is being all the more deeply impressed upon thoughtful natures by the events of the present war."

Columbus (O.) Journal : " The South did not stand alone at the bier of the dead Ensign who gave his life for his country. In the North the warmest sympathy was felt for the hero and his bereaved friends, lamenting his death, were nevertheless happy that he was called to the last muster under the flag that his father fought against in the late war. The sad event marked the complete reconciliation of the two sections."

New York Journal : " Ensign Bagley was a North Carolinian, son of a Confederate, and a Democrat. Admiral Dewey is a Vermonter, of politics which may be guessed at from the fact that he was simultaneously made an honorary member of the Union League and Democratic clubs. Lieutenant Hobson is an Alabanian and a Democrat. Surely this war obliterated sectionalism and partisanship in setting up the one standard of valor."

New York Times: " Ensign BAGLEY will be mourned as the first American victim of the war, but for that very reason he is sure of lasting remembrance. There is no American who does not remember the first victim of the civil war on the side of the Union. BAGLEY will be remembered as long as ELLSWORTH is remembered, but with the differene that whereas ELLSWORTH threw away his life in doing what he should have ordered to be done by others, BAGLEY laid down his in the strict line of his duty."

Denver (Col.) Times : " Deeply significant of the thorough restoration of our union is the fact that the first man to fall in the war with Spain is a Southerner. Ensign Bagley was from North Carolina, and was the son of a Confederate Major. He was born since the civil war, was a brilliant naval cadet, a gallant officer, and died smiling at danger, a worthy scion of the heroic people from whom he sprang.

" A more glorious death for a young officer could not be imagined. His blood was the final cement of a re-united nation, and will be an immortal landmark in history. As the first shot at Sumter rent the nation asunder, the long healing process was forever completed the moment he fell.

" Ellsworth, first heroic young officer to give up his life in the civil war, was the idol of the North. His name is remembered where generals and admirals and statesmen of the period are forgotten. But Bagley is the idol of the whole nation. Long after the pyramids of Egypt shall have sunk to the level of the Nile, his name will live in the memory of Americans."

Atlanta Constitution : " There is more than ordinary significance in the fact that the first drop of American blood shed in the present war with Spain should have come from the veins of one of North Carolina's gallant sons ; and if the anguish of private grief for one so gifted with the hero's spirit admits of any consolation, surely it is found in the gratifying fact that the blood of this young martyr freely spilled upon his country's altar, seals effectually the covenant of brotherhood between the North and the South and completes the work of reconciliation which commenced at Appomattox.

" While deploring with unaffected sorrow the tragic death of Ensign Bagley, North Carolina must feel some measure of patriotic pride in being the first State in the entire Union to suffer bereavement for the stars and stripes. But the whole South shares with North Carolina in the tearful honors of this initial sacrifice. Ensign Bagley illustrated in his ardent temperament the fire and spirit of the ideal Dixie youth. His father was one of the bravest soldiers who ever donned the Confederate uniform, and for generations back his ancestors were natives of the soil.

"More than any other influence which has operated to restore fraternity between the sections since the late war is the martyrdom of North Carolina's brave young officer. Eloquent speeches have softened the heart of the nation, but they have failed to approximate in welding and solidfying power the blood of Ensign Bagley."

Cincinnati Christian Advocate: "Twenty-seven years before, 24th, May, 1861, Elmer E. Ellsworth, colonel of the Fire Zouaves, of New York City, died in Alexandria, Virginia. In filial words to parents he had written: "Whatever may happen, cherish the consolation that I was engaged in the performance of a sacred duty." Ordered to Alexandria, his duty became the removal of the rebel flag that, from a window in the White House, Abraham Lincoln had seen floating defiance from the roof of the Marshall House. Fearless of death, Ellsworth cut the stars and bars from their staff—and died a martyr for the Union, the first soldier officer killed by secession arms.

"In no unworthy urns lie the dust of these young men. Born far apart one the son of the North, the other son of the South, they died beneath the same flag, and for the sacred cause of liberty. Had Bagley lived in '61, he might have fought beneath the eleven stars—but history had made him son of the Union, and he died, as Ellsworth died, for stars and stripes and the Fatherland.

"Beneath the Cuban sun he stood, his face full front toward the foreign foe; then fell for Cuba's freedom and philanthropy. When all the story of the struggle has been told—this also shall be told, that first to die in war for the Republic of Cuba, was Worth Bagley, ensign on the Winslow."

## CHAPTER XIV.

### TWO MONUMENTS.

TWO enduring monuments will tell the high esteem in which Ensign Bagley was held by the people and the permanent place that will be accorded him in history. On May 13th, the Raleigh News & Observer, in its local columns, said:

"Almost immediately upon the reception of the news of the battle here, Captain S. W. West, proposed a monument to the first martyr of the war for Cuban freedom, and indicated a willingness to start the subscription list with $100.

"Upon consideration, though, it was deemed best to build such a monument by popular subscriptions of from 1 cent to $5 each. This suggestion was endorsed by the other members of the committee, Mayor Russ, Mr. W. S. Primrose, Mr. R. T. Gray, Mr. F. A. Olds, who represented the city in honoring the dead hero. To this end they asked the press of the city to publish, from day to day, the list of subscribers, and to request patriotic citizens in this and other States to contribute to the fund."

On the same day the Raleigh Morning Post said:

"The universal sorrow at the death of Ensign Worth Bagley, the first officer in the American navy to fall in the war with Spain, finds expression in a spontaneous movement to contribute a fund for the erection of a monument to commemorate his gallant life and heroic death. To Mr. N. W. West, who followed the fortunes of the stars and bars during the war between the States, is due the credit of suggesting to the Morning Post that it undertake to raise a monument fund, and accordingly his name heads the list of subscribers. But the response of the public was so prompt that half a hundred citizens within half an hour, voluntarily came to the office and had their names enrolled.

"The monument fund will be raised by a plan that is truly a popular subscription. No subscriber will be permitted to contribute more than a dollar to the fund, while subscriptions for one cent, or for any sum more than one cent and not more than one dollar will be received. Subscriptions are solicited from patriotic citizens, wherever the American flag floats, who love their country and honor bravery. To this fund all can contribute, for the widow's mite or the child's penny will be acceptable as any man's dollar.

"The fund will be placed in the custody of the treasurer of the Post, and when a sufficient sum shall have been received, proper committees will make arrangements for the erection of a monument."

This fund which the Post thus inaugurated has grown so rapidly as to make it a bronze or marble statue, or monument erected in the city of Raleigh by contributions from all parts of the Union, will recall the story of the valor of Worth Bagley to all visitors to his native city, and be a daily inspiration to the youth of his native state.

A monument of another character, one peculiarly fitting, will connect his name forever in history with Cushing, Ericcson, Winslow [also a native of North Carolina] and other heroes of the American Navy. On the 20th of June, 1898, the Secretary of the Navy announced in the public press that the first of the new torpedo boats to go into commission would bear the name of the brave young Ensign Bagley, the first American officer to lose his life in this war. Hon. Richmond Pearson member of the House of Representatives of the ninth North Carolina district, conveyed the information of this honor in the following telegram from Washington, D. C., to a relative of the dead Ensign:

"The Secretary of the Navy has just told me he would name the new torpedo boat 'Worth Bagley.' When I described the spontaneous outpouring at Bagley's funeral, the Secretary said: 'It was well deserved.'"

The press and the public received this action with approval. The following editorial from the Syracuse, N Y. Post voiced this sentiment that found expression everywhere:

"It was a deserved act of grateful recognition for the Government to give the name of Bagley to the first of the new torpedo boats to be constructed. This brave young officer, the first commissioned officer in the Navy to fall in the war, met death under peculiarly heroic circumstances. He did his duty at a most perilous post, exhibiting a bravery and heroism worthy of a veteran officer. The honor due to his memory will be an inspiration to other young officers that emulate his virtues."

## TWO MOTHERS.

[Written by Mr. W. C. Ervin on the Death of Ensign Worth Bagley.]

Two mothers stand by a hero's grave
  In a Southern city fair.
And one sheds tears for the fallen brave,
  And cries in her dark despair;
But one makes never a cry nor moan,
  And stands in her pride elate;
For one is the mother of flesh and bone,
  And one is the mother State.

O, mother, you of the burning tears
  And you of the dark despair,
The hope and pride of your love-lit years
  Are shrouded and buried there:
For fame is naught when the loved are dead,
  And a nation's praise is vain
When the parting words at the grave are said,
  And the soul is seared with pain.

And, mother, you in your pride elate,
  You joy that another name
Is blazoned now on the lofty gate
  In the temple of your fame;
"Behold!" you cry, "on wave or strand,
  How my children die for me—
They fall like Spartans on the land
  And like Vikings on the sea!"

A stately shaft of enduring stone
  One mother will rear in pride,
And with sculptor's chisel for aye make known
  How a Carolinian died!
And one will plant the cypress tree
  To sigh for the deadly strife,
And a rose, as white as the snow can be,
  To tell of a spotless life.

One mother brings, as a last farewell,
  To our hero's grave to-day,
The amaranth and the asphodel,
  And one a garland of bay;
And one stands there in her grief alone,
  And one in her pride elate—
For one is the mother of flesh and bone,
  And one is the mother State.

www.ingramcontent.com/pod-product-compliance
Lightning Source LLC
Chambersburg PA
CBHW021946160426
43195CB00011B/1248